THE INNOCENCE MACHINE

THE INNOCENCE SYSTEM GONE HAYWIRE

STEVE SCARBOROUGH

Genius
Book Publishing

The Innocence Machine

Published by:
Genius Book Publishing
PO Box 250380
Milwaukee Wisconsin 53225 USA
GeniusBookPublishing.com
GeniusTrueCrime.com

ISBN: 978-1-970450-08-8
260515 HQ

CONTENTS

DISCLAIMER

This book reflects the opinions, interpretations, and professional observations of the author based upon publicly available records, court documents, media reporting, investigative materials, and forensic analysis. Any conclusions regarding the guilt, innocence, or involvement of individuals discussed herein are expressions of opinion protected under the First Amendment and are not presented as definitive statements of fact unless established by a court of law. The author acknowledges that reasonable individuals may interpret the same evidence differently, and readers are encouraged to draw their own conclusions.

CHAPTER 1

SOME INITIAL THOUGHTS

***The Innocence Machine*: A new approach to true crime cases under scrutiny.**

THE INNOCENCE PROJECT, AND MANY OF ITS chapters and similar organizations around the country, are dedicated to bringing justice to those people incarcerated who they feel are innocent. While this is a noble purpose, a closer examination of their cases can quickly muddy the waters. Many factors from multiple factions outside the criminal justice system influence and alter the outcomes of these cases, while the quest for actual innocence is lost and corrupted. Many times, this comes with disastrous and deadly results, sometimes costing the lives of those involved along with the people they are trying to exonerate.

Walking a tightrope between the positive and negative aspects of innocence campaigns, *The Innocence Machine* shows both sides of the fight to exonerate wrongly convicted people and delves into the oversaturation of the innocence craze. It exposes the truth behind these external investigations that derail the criminal justice system and can cause the release of dangerous criminals back into society.

The innocence system is broken. It has gotten way off track. The Innocence Machine is a product of that broken system.

In this book, you will take a deep dive into some of these innocence programs, and, along the way, will be able to examine the murders that prompted the calls for the innocence of these convicted criminals. This book highlights numerous true crime cases, examining the details, why innocence organizations promoted the convicted person's innocence, and the results of their actions.

Innocence programs typically try to address the flaws in the justice system, but this book addresses the weaknesses in innocence programs. The concept behind *The Innocence Machine* is that the innocence craze raises many questions and concerns about how innocence advocates select cases and how those cases are investigated.

In a very revealing statement made by a defense attorney on a *Dateline* program, Bob Dudek said, "In my 22, 23 years of being an appellate defense attorney, [name redacted] is the only one of about two or possibly three people I genuinely believed was innocent."

If you follow true crime, watch any of the multiple true crime documentaries available on streaming channels, and have any tendency to believe in a convicted person's innocence, this book is for you.

The Innocence Project has evolved into a craze that is

becoming an Innocence Machine, and it appears to be based on the assumption that almost everyone who has been convicted could be innocent. Incomplete reinvestigations of cases are often conducted by individuals untrained in detective work and investigation, where bias and the omission of pertinent evidence are common, leading to disastrous consequences.

It is essential that there is accountability and separation from the Innocence Project. The Innocence Project provides valuable and commendable work. However, the Innocence Machine is the craze to seek out and uncover innocent, convicted people, sometimes without thoroughly vetting the case. This can be based on the media and public innocence campaigns. As seen in the example of the Porter case, featured within, it is sometimes based on the machinations of the convicts themselves. Once the Innocence Machine gets started, it rolls away, unstoppable and out of control.

The Porter case demands that all innocence cases be viewed with extreme skepticism. The actions that occurred post-conviction demonstrates that siren calls for attention can lead to inappropriate conduct. They can also lead to ignoring specific facts to reach the point of innocence, as seen in many other cases reviewed throughout this book.

The Porter case, along with several others, is one in which the convict initiated and controlled the narrative; there are others in which the public controlled it, and still others in which the media, at times, controlled it, when it would seem that the actual innocence organizations should be steering the narrative.

In almost all the cases presented in this book, crucial

inculpatory evidence is ignored or dismissed by the innocence activists to present the convicted person as innocent. Innocence activists sometimes seem to overlook specific pieces of evidence and instead focus on ambiguous evidence, which can lead to a misrepresentation of the facts. Also, they often lack the investigative skills required for a thorough, unbiased investigation. Oddly enough, it seems they frequently accuse the police of the same thing. A common refrain from defense attorneys is that the police had tunnel vision and ignored other suspects. Are innocence advocates using that same tunnel vision after they see publicity suggesting a convicted person's innocence, and are they ignoring crucial and incriminating evidence indicating their guilt?

Familiarity with the defendant or convicted person appears to be a factor in how people perceive the case, especially if that defendant is a famous person. It has often been said that everyone in prison claims to be innocent, and many of them are likable and persuasive. Are those lawyers and innocence activists who visit the people in prison or interview the defendant's family more susceptible to thinking that they are innocent?

One way that defendants and innocence activists draw the attention of innocence organizations is by promoting their concerns through a marketing strategy that utilizes signage and local protests, as well as more widely through websites and media attention.

With every single one of the cases reviewed in this book, there is a vast discrepancy between the evidence presented at trial and the re-creation presented on the call-for-innocence websites. In fact, it is difficult to find the actual evidence in these cases because so many entries are biased in favor of the defendants, even by legitimate media outlets. The language used can be very persuasive, but it always gets in the way. For example, in the Marcellas Williams case, discussed in more detail later, almost none of the media entries list all the inculpatory evidence pointing to Williams.

Proof of innocence is vague and disjointed. It feels very subjective at times. These cases create an enigma. Would you rather a guilty man goes free or an innocent man not? It is easy to fall into the mind game of who is really innocent. Many of these cases feature people who are hardened criminals and hardly innocent in their past crimes. Steven Avery (discussed next) could be an example of that.

MAKING A MURDERER: AN INCOMPLETE DOCUMENTARY FILM

Many recent documentaries have exploited the convicted person as the innocent victim of the justice system. This is evident in such cases as the Laci Peterson murder case (discussed later). There is a tendency to conveniently overlook crucial incriminating evidence for the sake of a gripping story. One production that follows the model of the wrongfully convicted innocent person is the 2015 Netflix documentary *Making a Murderer*.

Making a Murderer is a compelling and engaging view of the 2005 murder of Teresa Halbach. The film is an excellent true crime documentary, featuring all the required elements of police corruption, tainted evidence, false confessions, tunnel vision, and, of course, a wrongly convicted person.

Making a Murderer won several well-deserved awards, including four Emmy awards in 2016. With the first scene, the film hooks the audience, eager to see what happens next. The "murderer" is Steven Avery, and through many on-screen interviews, his demeanor is so convincing that, as a viewer, one really believes his side of the case. Since Avery was previously wrongly convicted of another crime, the documentary is successful in making the viewer sincerely doubt his guilt in the Halbach murder and think he was railroaded once again.

If perhaps the creator of *Making a Murderer* thought they were following in the footsteps of the *Thin Blue Line* (discussed later), a review of the actual evidence shows otherwise. This was Hollywood-type moviemaking. Numerous websites and books, including one by the prosecution, address the incriminating evidence left out of the film. Upon analyzing all the evidence, it becomes clear why the jury reached its guilty verdict. In fact, despite *Making A Murderer* presenting scenes suggesting that Avery's cousin was completely innocent, it is easy to see his culpability in the crimes that occurred at the wreckage yard in Wisconsin.

If the purpose is to create controversy, these documentaries can be very effective, as they possess tremendous power to change people's minds or generate specific thoughts. But if it turns out that they didn't present all the evidence, then what is the value? Do they end up merely like a horror movie, accomplishing their goal of creating emotion and controversy? Or are they essentially empty?

Then they become a noble quest worthy of admiration and respect without any payoff.

A Fully Complete Incriminating Case

Due to the documentary series, *Making a Murderer*, first released in 2015, many people still believe Steven Avery is innocent of the heinous crime he committed. Innocence advocates have called for his exoneration.

One can suppose that Steven Avery, once released from prison on a wrongful conviction for a 1984 sexual assault, must have thought he was invincible. That he could commit a murder in his front yard, of a woman he had called to his house, and get away with it.

A photographer for *Autotrader* magazine was declared missing after she failed to check in with her employer following an appointment on October 31, 2005. It was discovered that Teresa Halbach had an appointment on the grounds of Avery's Auto Salvage to photograph a minivan. The police immediately responded to the auto salvage yard and began a search, assisted by volunteers, including law enforcement personnel and local residents.

Halbach's car was eventually found by searchers, partially covered by brush, at the very back of the salvage yard. This discovery led to a thorough search of the vast salvage yard, including the area where Halbach was supposed to meet the caller who had requested a photograph of the minivan. It was learned that the vehicle belonged to Steven Avery's sister.

It was also discovered that Steven Avery had previously had Halbach respond to his residence on the property for a photograph, and that Halbach had asked not to ever respond to any of Avery's future requests. She told her boss that she was uncomfortable with Avery as he had opened the door in a towel. Avery may have known this because, during the call to *Autotrader*, he provided another name and address; however, the caller, who had used Star 67 to conceal his phone number, had specifically requested Teresa Halbach.

After researching Avery's background, the police reviewed his record. Avery had been convicted of burglary in 1981 and had served 10 months in jail. In 1982, Avery burned his cat in a bonfire and was convicted of animal cruelty. Avery was also accused by the wife of a Manitowoc County officer of exposing himself to her as she was driving in Manitowoc.

In 1985, Avery threatened his cousin with a gun and threatened to kill her for telling people he had been flagellating himself on his front lawn. He was convicted and sentenced to six years for "endangering safety while evincing a depraved mind" and possession of a firearm by a felon.

Steven Avery was arrested in November 2005 and charged with the murder of Teresa Halbach. During the trial, the evidence discovered in Halbach's vehicle and a search of Avery's property were presented. Investigators had found incriminating evidence from Halbach's vehicle, Avery's bedroom in his house, Avery's garage, and the front- and back-yards of Avery's property.

Halbach's bent license plates were found along one of the long roads between stacks of damaged automobiles on the salvage yard property. Her vehicle was found on a rise along the very rear of the yard, partially hidden by wood and branches.

The car was searched and processed for evidence. Teresa Halbach's DNA was found in the trunk area of the vehicle. Steven Avery's blood was found in the interior on the ignition, on a CD case, and on the seats of the vehicle. Avery's touch DNA, most likely from sweat, was found in numerous places in the car and on the hood latch. The CSI unit processed the hood latch because Avery's nephew, Brandon Dassey, said in interviews that Avery always disconnected the battery when he brought new cars into the yard.

Brandon Dassey was also charged in the Halbach case after he confessed to helping Avery kill Halbach and dispose of her body. Even though the confession, as shown in *Making a Murderer*, revealed that police conducted the interrogation improperly, Dassey did provide critical information that led to the police discovering significant evidence. He told them about the battery on her vehicle, he told them about the shooting in the garage and using the rifle from Avery's bedroom, and about the disposal of the body on Avery's property. Dassey refused to testify at Avery's trial but testified at his own trial and never mentioned any police coercion. Brandon Dassey was convicted of complicity in the murder in a separate trial.

During the trial, Avery's attorneys focused on the blood evidence from Halbach's vehicle (deflecting away from his touch DNA) and presented a vial of Avery's blood with a puncture hole visible in the stopper, speculating the blood was extracted and place in the vehicle by law enforcement, as part of the defense's overall case of Avery being framed by police.

However, the prosecution presented testimony by FBI technicians who tested the blood recovered from Halbach's car for EDTA, a preservative that is used in blood vials for blood collection, and found it was not present. Therefore, it was not blood from that vial.

Based upon the previous handling of Avery's assault case, and because Avery sued Manitowoc County, the Manitowoc County department ceded control of the murder investigation to the neighboring Calumet County Sheriff's Department.

Investigators learned from Avery's cousins that he had had a bonfire that night on his property. Dassy also told police that he had seen Avery burn some girl's clothes in the fire. They then searched a burn pit near Avery's home and found bone fragments that were later identified as Halbach's. In a burn barrel near the burn pit, investigators found Halbach's damaged phone, her camera, and her Personal Digital Assistant.

As a result of the search of Avery's home, they found a .22 rifle stored above his bed and spots of dried blood in his bathroom. Upon a subsequent search of Avery's bedroom, they found Halbach's car keys hidden behind a bookcase. They photographed the keys, not exactly where they found them, which would have been difficult to do, but on the floor below the bookcase. The car keys were tested, and Avery's DNA was located on them.

Dassey also told investigators that Halbach had been shot with the .22, and police researched the garage and found a bullet that was fired from Avery's rifle with Halbach's DNA, from passing through her body.

Interestingly, the defense focused on the blood evidence as being planted by the police. However, even if that was possible, how did the police obtain Avery's sweat or skin cells for his DNA on the vehicle and the keys found in Avery's bedroom? The film successfully promoted the evidence-planting allegations by using blood evidence, but skipped informing the audience about finding Avery's transfer DNA within the victim's vehicle.

Following the release of the *Making a Murderer* documentary, over 120,000 petition signatures were gathered and sent to the White House, calling for Avery's release.

Steven Avery had previously been released from prison on September 11, 2003, after serving 18 years for a 1985 wrongful sexual assault conviction. He was exonerated by DNA evidence.

Avery's case gained widespread attention from innocence activists and the media. The Republican chairman of the Wisconsin Assembly established a task force to reduce the likelihood of wrongful convictions. A bill known as the Avery Bill was passed in 2005 to reform the criminal justice system.

However, many people did cry foul over *Making a Murderer's* depiction of the case. The prosecutors on the case wrote a book, *Avery: The Case Against Steven Avery and What* Making a Murderer *Gets Wrong, published in 2017.* Numerous websites address the documentary, including *14 pieces of troubling evidence that Making a Murderer left out, Here's What Was Left Out of Making a Murderer,* and

Making a Murderer: Key Pieces Of Evidence The Show Leaves Out.

Due to the mountain of evidence, including DNA evidence, Avery was convicted of the murder of Teresa Halbach and remains in prison today.

It seems that the public has a never-ending thirst for stories about the broken justice system, police corruption, and the conviction of innocent people. It takes a concerted effort to cut through the noise and find the truth.

The innocence movement coincides with the vast interest in true crime. In this age of the never-ending public appetite for true crime, have we become incapable of objective thought, of reviewing the evidence from an impersonal clinical perspective? Are we too concerned with who the good guys are and who the bad guys are? Making situations too black-and-white rather than accepting the nuances that occur in real life?

As you read through the cases in the rest of this book and learn more about innocence campaigns and their tactics in trying to establish innocence, maybe you'll understand why more scrutiny and skepticism are necessary. You will also learn the formula and strategy that the Innocence Machine uses to facilitate its program. And perhaps the next time you watch a true crime documentary, you'll be able to be more impartial and cautious in your conclusions.

Kills His Savior

On June 10, 2010, Miami-Dade 911 received a frantic call

from a man claiming that his girlfriend had tried to kill herself.

The caller was Yathomas Riley, a professional boxer. When paramedics arrived at the apartment in Homestead, Florida, they found 31-year-old Koketia King unconscious on her bed. She had a bullet wound in her leg and had been shot in the face. Blood was around the room, and Riley also had blood on his clothes. Riley told police that his sometime girlfriend and the mother of his child had shot herself in a jealous rage.

When police responded to the hospital to talk to Koketia King, they observed she had extensive damage to her head, and doctors said that she would have permanent facial impairment. After she regained consciousness, she told police that Riley purposely shot her. Riley said he was innocent and did not shoot his girlfriend.

At the scene, the police found two spent bullets and two casings. Because King had three wounds, she thought she had been shot three times. Doctors at Jackson Memorial Hospital deduced from her injuries that she had only been shot twice, as one bullet had entered above her left buttock and exited her left thigh, and another bullet had entered her face. Some people would later see this as important in the case.

Yathomas Riley would be arrested based on the charge by King that he had shot her. Riley was adamant that he was innocent. Koketia King was a corrections officer at the Dade Correctional Institution in Florida City, and the police determined that the weapon was hers.

Riley had been an amateur boxer who had a string of successful fights when he met King at a family reunion.

They soon moved in together, and King became pregnant around Christmas 2005. Their son was born in September 2006. They then moved to California so Riley could train for a fight.

Eventually, Riley obtained a professional contract with a promoter in New York, and around that time, King and their son moved back to Florida. Riley and King entered into a long-distance relationship.

Riley met Lisa Amodio, a medical student, at his training gym in New York, and they became friends. Soon, Amodio was working in Riley's corner as a cut person. As a pro, Riley was also a successful fighter, going 4-0 in his first year. Riley and Lisa Amodio became engaged in 2009, which, of course, upset Koketia King.

When Riley moved back to South Florida to train for a fight at the Seminole Hard Rock Hotel & Casino, he stayed with King at her apartment in Homestead, Florida.

In June 2009, police responded to King's apartment and arrested Riley for molesting King's 12-year-old daughter. After an investigation, police had doubts about the statement from King's daughter, and the prosecutors subsequently dropped the charges.

Riley returned to New York for more successful fights, but in June 2010, he visited King in Florida. During this visit, Riley stated that he discovered a letter indicating King was assisting inmates in filing tax returns with falsified information, which led to an argument between the two. (Koketia King has never been charged with any crime.) That is when the shooting took place.

While Riley was being held in jail on this attempted murder charge, several people began showing support for his innocence. Lisa Amodio made public statements about his innocence in the case. She was even on the local TV news professing his innocence. The Cryon below her name on the TV news said, "Riley's Fiancé said King was shot twice, once in the buttocks and once in the face."

The fact that she was shot twice seemed to support King's statement, and not Riley's claim that she shot herself, as who would shoot themselves in the leg before shooting themselves in the face? There were several statements by Riley's supporters that mentioned King had changed her story multiple times. Of course, it was possible that being shot in the head had disrupted her memory.

As often happens in innocence-craze cases, and as you will see throughout this book, often the benefit of the doubt is not given to the victim but to the defendant. All of King's statements were dismissed as lies rather than as the result of confusion.

There was an extensive "Free Riley" campaign, and one of Riley's supporters was *Miami New Times*, which published articles suggesting that King's statements were unreliable and that the tax letter showed it. Investigators reviewed the case, and on August 17, 2012, Yathomas Riley was released.

Riley and Amodio eventually settled into a large house in Leesburg, Georgia, in August 2013. They were married in April 2015 and had a son together in the fall of that year. Lisa was an emergency room physician, and Riley ran a car repair business and opened Riley's Boxing Gym.

On June 14, 2015, Lisa Amodio Riley, now 34, was found unconscious inside her Leesburg home. She filed a complaint against her husband, stating he had assaulted her and threatened her with a gun, and Yathomas was arrested.

He was charged with battery and assault and ordered to stay away from Lisa and to give up his firearms to the police. He maintained his innocence. Riley was released on bond.

On July 9, 2015, while Yathomas was still out on bail for the assault charge, he made a 911 call to report that his wife, Lisa, had shot herself. Lisa was pronounced dead at the scene. Riley was arrested on the prior domestic assault charge, and police began investigating the shooting death. Police later believed Yathomas had shot and murdered his wife.

During the murder trial for Yathomas Riley, the prosecution closed their arguments by stating that Yathomas had killed Lisa on July 9, 2015, while she was on her knees.

On June 24th, 2016, Thomas Riley was found guilty of the murder of Lisa Amodio-Riley, and he was sentenced to lifetime imprisonment without parole.

It seems that the woman who believed in his innocence, who had campaigned for his release, had eventually been murdered by him. This is a perfect example of the emotional attachment that is a component of the Innocence Machine — fullhearted faith in the innocence of a convicted person.

CHAPTER 2
QUESTIONS ABOUT INNOCENCE CAMPAIGNS AND INNOCENCE PROJECTS

Is the Yathomas Riley case an example of the innocence craze gone haywire? Did the media and Riley's own wife fall for the lure of the call for innocence?

Are people unable to resist the call for the innocence of a "wrongly convicted" person? Are people unable to resist a downtrodden person who avows and proclaims their innocence? Is the thought of a person possibly being unjustly incarcerated for a crime they claim they did not commit so tantalizing that people must pursue it?

Is the media unable to resist a story about a "wrongly convicted" person? Are stories about a person sitting in jail for "a crime they did not commit" so compelling that the media must pursue them?

The Innocence Machine seems to run on the assumption that almost everyone who has been convicted is really innocent. They just need to find the proof.

Cases like Caldwell's (discussed next) and Funches' (discussed later) raise troubling questions about innocence organizations and the lengths to which top lawyers are willing to go to free a man convicted of murder.

There is a massive chasm between minimal evidence and innocence. Many criminal cases do not have all the answers to the crime. Many cases rely on minimal evidence and circumstantial evidence to complete the investigation. In fact, almost no case has all the facts. It is rare for anyone to know precisely what happened in most crimes. Because there is minimal evidence that may raise questions about the case or the perpetrator does not automatically mean the person is innocent.

Interestingly, criminal justice terminology defines direct evidence as only eyewitness testimony and classifies all other evidence, including fingerprints and DNA, as circumstantial. However, according to Innocence Project statistics, most exonerations of convicted people have, at their core, mistaken eyewitness testimony.

CHAPTER 3

FALSE WITNESS TO AN INNOCENCE PROJECT (INNOCENCE LAWYER MISCONDUCT?)

Convicted murderer Marritte Funches says he lied to help get another convicted murderer, Maurice Caldwell, exonerated by the Northern California Innocence Project.

Maurice Caldwell was convicted of murder in 1991 for a drug deal killing that occurred in San Francisco, CA. On June 30, 1990, a woman named Judy Acosta was shot to death on the street during an apparent drug deal that went sour in a public housing project in San Francisco.

Police did a neighborhood canvas for witnesses and found a woman, Mary Cobb, living in the area, who said she saw Maurice Caldwell the night of the shooting. She identified Caldwell as one of the gunmen.

Police took Caldwell to trial in March 1991 in San Francisco County Superior Court. Caldwell was convicted of murder and sentenced to life in prison without parole, primarily based on the testimony of Mary Cobb.

Within the next several years, the Northern California Innocence Project (NCIP) took up Caldwell's cause, and a new lawyer, Paige Keneb, took the case. The Project obtained information suggesting that the actual gunmen might be Marritte Funches and Henry Martin. The NCIP and Keneb located Funches in prison in Nevada, where he was serving a life sentence for the murder of a Reno, NV, cab driver, which he committed after the Acosta case. It later turned out that Caldwell, who knew Funches from their neighborhood, had been communicating with him while both were in prison.

Paige Keneb began visiting Funches in prison. Eventually, Funches, a friend of Caldwell's, gave a sworn statement claiming he had committed the crime with another person, not Caldwell. The NCIP appealed the case and obtained a hearing in 2010 to attempt to overturn the conviction.

Prior to the hearing, Funches also helped Keneb find several additional witnesses who said that Caldwell did not commit the Acosta murder. However, those witnesses demanded anonymity.

Based on this new evidence, in March 2010, a San Francisco Superior Court judge granted Caldwell a new trial, ruling that he had been denied effective counsel since they had not pursued these other witnesses. Caldwell was released from prison, and the NCIP declared another victory. This success centered upon Funches' confession and these new witnesses. This release is still celebrated on the Innocence Project websites and the National Registry of Exonerations.

The District Attorney declined to refile the case against Caldwell and dismissed it. Paige Kaneb, the NCIP, and supporters welcomed Caldwell upon his release on March 28, 2011. It later turned out that

Kaneb had even let Caldwell stay at her apartment for a time.

After Caldwell was released from prison, he sued the city of San Francisco for a civil rights violation. The lawyers defending the city in the lawsuit uncovered several inconsistencies in the witnesses' stories, especially after the witnesses were told they could no longer remain anonymous. The witnesses were reinterviewed, and the city attorneys accused Kaneb of "manipulating the facts" in a filing, according to a *San Francisco Standard* article. Additionally, Caldwell lost a 2018 court ruling to have him declared factually innocent. Despite this new evidence, in 2021, the San Francisco Board of Supervisors approved an $8 million settlement for Caldwell.

The *San Francisco Standard* published an article, titled "A Jailhouse Romance, a Recanted Murder Confession, and Broken Promises," on June 10, 2024, with a number of details about the case and the relationship between Kaneb and Funches. They uncovered a number of texts and photographs between the two, including a conversation in which it appears Funches and Keneb admitted to lying about Caldwell. The article presents a December 2023 conversation with Kaneb, in which Funches said she told him he lied about Caldwell's innocence.

Funches eventually came forward publicly, and admitted he had lied to help Kaneb and the NCIP get Caldwell released. According to the *Standard* article, he now said Kaneb knew about his lie but continued to represent the case publicly as an exoneration.

This is a clear case of a person falsely confessing to a crime they did not commit to help someone get released from prison and support an innocence organization in its quest. It also seems possible that the person working with the Innocence Project (NCIP) engaged in some inappropriate behavior. If this has happened once, has it happened in other cases? Have other convicted individuals been released by Innocence Project organizations despite being genuinely guilty?

Innocence System Spun out of Control, Egregious Conduct by an Innocence Campaign

A Murder in the Park should be required viewing for every innocence organization, law school, and college innocence program. Much of the following information is from this documentary and Chicago news sources. Follow this case closely, as it has many twists and turns.

A Murder in the Park is a 2014 documentary that explores the conviction and subsequent release of Anthony Porter. Porter was sentenced in 1983 for the shooting deaths of two teenagers. Porter was freed from prison after Professor David Protess, founder of the Medill Innocence Project, and a group of his journalism students at Northwestern University examined the case. The professor and his students brought forward another suspect who was eventually convicted. The filmmakers contend that Protess and his students misrepresented and fabricated evidence, resulting in the conviction of another "innocent" man, Alstory Simon, in 2011. The professor and his students were wrong about almost everything.

On August 15, 1982, at about 1 a.m., several people

were in the pool area of Washington Park, swimming and relaxing after a large celebration and parade earlier along nearby Martin Luther King Drive in the South Side of Chicago. Two young people, 18-year-old Jerry Hillard and 19-year-old Marilyn Green, sat in the bleachers that overlooked the pool. A man who had also been seated near the couple in the bleachers stood up and shot both Green and Hillard and then ran away from them and toward the rear of the pool area.

Marilyn Green was shot through her hand and into her neck. Hilliard was shot twice in the head, once almost right between his eyes and once in his forehead.

Green actually got up from the bleachers, walked out of the pool area past some responding officers, and was then helped into a police car. The Chicago officer drove her to a hospital. She later died while being treated.

Responding officers, who first confronted a bleeding Green, then saw a man running from behind the bleachers. One officer stopped and frisked the man, but didn't find a weapon, and released him. The officer would be able to subsequently identify the man he stopped.

The wounded Hillard was also still alive, and police helped him down from the bleachers and tried to treat him. He was also taken to the hospital, and he also died.

That early morning, the witnesses at the pool were Henry Williams, William Taylor, Eugene Beckwith, Mark Senior, Kenneth Edwards, and Michael Woodfork. They all identified Porter because they knew him from the neighborhood. A police officer also put Porter behind the pool area, where Porter ran away from the scene.

Henry Williams and William Taylor had gone to the

Washington Park pool to swim. Williams said that after swimming, he got out of the pool, and Porter came up to him and asked for money, putting a gun to his head. Williams replied that he didn't have any, but Porter took some cash out of Williams' pocket and then walked away. Williams said he saw Porter go up into the bleachers and sit by a couple already sitting up there.

Taylor said he was still swimming, got out of the pool, and heard a shot. Taylor said he turned and looked up into the bleachers and saw Porter shoot the male victim twice. Standing near the end of the pool, he saw Porter run right past him and out of the area. Taylor was one eyewitness to the actual killing.

There were other witnesses at the pool that morning. Kenneth Edwards and Eugene Beckwith were also in the pool area, and they saw Porter sitting up in the bleachers with another man sitting by the couple. They knew it was Porter because they knew him from the neighborhood. The two friends were swimming at the far end of the pool when they heard the shooting; they looked in that direction. Eugene Beckwith said he saw a person stand up and shoot the couple. Beckwith became the second witness to see the shooting, but he wasn't wholly sure that Porter had fired the gun. In the area where Edwards was standing, he had an unobstructed view of the bleachers. Edwards testified that he actually saw Porter fire the weapon at the victims. Edwards became the third person to see the shooting. The two men quickly left by jumping over the fence. They fled because they said Porter knew them and they feared him.

Two other witnesses who were there that morning

were Mark Senior and Michael Woodfork. They said they saw three men and one woman up in the bleachers. They said one of the men was Anthony Porter. They were sure because they knew him from the neighborhood.

Based on all the eyewitness identifications, including Taylor's identification of Porter in a lineup and the police officer's identification of Porter as the person he stopped right after the incident, Anthony Porter was arrested on August 15, 1982.

At Porter's trial in 1983, Henry Williams and William Taylor testified that they saw Porter up in the bleachers. Williams testified that Porter had robbed him at gunpoint and then saw him go up in the bleachers. Taylor testified that it was Porter he saw murder the couple. One of the responding officers also testified that it was Porter that they stopped and frisked after they saw him running away from the pool area.

In the trial's penalty phase, two more witnesses testified, Earl Lewis and Douglas McGhee. Lewis testified that before the murders, he got into a confrontation with Porter. They were arguing about Porter kicking his dog, and Porter put a gun to Lewis' head and shot, but Lewis was able to move his head slightly, and he was only wounded by the bullet. He said that if he didn't move, he most likely would be dead. McGhee said that Porter had once beaten him and robbed him in the very same bleachers as the murders.

For the defense, one of Porter's friends testified that he and Porter were drinking together at the time of the murders.

The jury found Anthony Porter guilty of the murders

of Marilyn Green and Jerry Hilliard, and he was sentenced to death.

This was not a case of stranger identification. All six witnesses, Henry Williams, William Taylor, Eugene Beckwith, Mark Senior, Kenneth Edwards, and Michael Woodfork, knew Anthony Porter. The responding police officer also identified Porter.

Sometime around 1998, journalists and their professor, David Protess, at the Medill Journalism School at Northwestern University, began investigating the Green and Hillard murders. The professor may have directed the students to people on death row and to Anthony Porter, perhaps since the crime occurred locally in Chicago. The students began working on the Porter case and reviewing the available summaries.

The students in the professor's class went to the site of the murders, Washington Park, Chicago. They developed what they saw as conflicting evidence from the original police reports and that of one witness, William Taylor. The students believed that the sight lines in the pool area contradicted the witness' statement. They believed that due to metal obstructions in the pool area, the witness could not have clearly seen the murder. This seemed to suggest that the witness was mistaken and added fuel to the notion that Porter was innocent.

Once the innocence case was in full swing, Northwestern and Protess promoted it widely, and most media analyses presented a very different case from the prosecution's. The media was getting information from the school program, not court records.

In what seems like a typical case of overfamiliarity

breeding mistakes, the students interviewed Porter in prison on two separate occasions in December 1998 He told them he was innocent, and they believed in his innocence. This is a common occurrence and has been observed in many other high-profile innocence cases, such as the JonBenét Ramsey case (discussed later in this book), in which journalists embedded with the people of interest tend to lean toward their innocence. The students said Porter was very convincing when he claimed to be innocent.

The Northwestern students concluded after visiting the Washington Park pool that the witness, Taylor, couldn't have seen the murder because of obstructions in the pool area. If the victims were in the far corner, the angle prevented the witness from seeing the act. It turned out that the students thought that the shooting took place in the corner of the bleachers, but it actually took place more in the center of the bleachers, which can be verified by viewing the actual crime scene photos. It was also determined from the photos that the metal posts the students thought were obstructing the witness' view were not present in 1982. The students also believed it would have been too dark to see anything that early morning. However, crime scene photos conflict with this opinion. It also turned out that there were other eyewitnesses to the actual shooting besides William Taylor. However, the media was informed that Porter had been wrongly convicted.

Northwestern students interviewed William Taylor in 1999. A private investigator (PI) and a student spoke with Taylor and informed him that his identification was incorrect. Taylor said that he was convinced by the PI and a student that maybe he was wrong about seeing the shooting. Taylor said, “Maybe I did make a mistake, but I don’t think I did.” They gave him a written statement to sign to record him saying he did not see the murder. They had him say, “I did not see Anthony Porter shoot anyone.” This was used as his recantation.

In the affidavit prepared for the witness by the PI at that meeting, it said, “I was present at the park when the shooting occurred. I did not see Anthony Porter shoot anybody. I never saw Anthony Porter with a gun. I did not see who shot the victims that day.” What was not present in the affidavit or recording was that Taylor had testified that he had definitely seen Porter run by him right after the shooting.

When Taylor was later interviewed, he said he just wanted them to go away and end this case for him. He said he never recanted, and that conversation was misconstrued. Taylor also stated he believed that Porter was guilty.

The information released to the media was that there was only one single witness to the murders and that that witness had recanted. The Protess team and the PI told the media that the only surviving witness (one of the six had since died) was now recanting his testimony, implying that no remaining evidence existed against Porter. Therefore, Porter was innocent.

In a TV interview, Protess stated that the police began with the assumption that Porter was guilty and constructed a case around that. “They railroaded him.” Protess stated that they had an objective view and did not have an agenda. However, when a student was asked in a grand jury deposition, they said that they felt the assignment was to "find evidence that would lead to freeing this man."

The main problem with Protess' Northwestern presentation was that he and his students believed that there was only one witness who fingered Porter. They thought the witness had recanted, leaving no witness to say Porter committed the crime. The media picked up on this and reported it.

Protess' team got information from the mother of one of the victims that she suspected a man named Alstory Simon, because Simon and his family had moved away right after the murders. But Simon's mother said he had come home about 7 p.m. The murder didn't take place until 1 a.m.

In 1999, Anthony Porter provided the Protess team with the name Walter Jackson as someone to contact. Jackson then signed an affidavit for them that Simon had told him he had shot the couple in the bleachers. They had also been given the name of Inez Jackson as someone to contact. The students interviewed Inez Jackson, Walter's aunt, and she said she had been present at the scene of the crime, and it was Simon who had done the killing. Inez said that she was up in the bleachers, making that two men and two women who were there. Inez also said that it was early in the evening, not 1 a.m. Inez Jackson's and Walter Jackson's statements became part of the Protess team's presentation to request Porter's release.

The team then focused on Alstory Simon. After Simon was pressured by the team's PI and an imposing partner who questioned him at his home, he confessed. The confession was videotaped. This quickly led to Simon's arrest. To get the confession, the PI showed Simon a video with an actor saying that he knew Simon had committed the crime, and then showed him a video of Protess and a video of Inez Jackson, both claiming that he had committed the murder. This all contributed to Simon confessing to the crime. Simon would later say that the PI rehearsed him on precisely what to say in the video confession.

An investigation panel was formed, and the panel decided that Porter was innocent, that the witness was inaccurate, and that a man named Simon was really guilty. The panel may have been influenced by the details Protess and the Medill Innocence Project had presented. The Northwestern presentation included the testimony of the one witness who recanted, the affidavits of Inez Jackson and Walter Jackson, and the video of Alstory Simon's confession recorded by Protess' PI. Simon's confession video was released to the media and widely broadcast, and two days later, the State's Attorney had Porter released.

Simon was arrested, and an attorney contacted him for representation. The attorney convinced Simon to confess and plead guilty to spare him the death penalty. After pleading guilty, Simon was convicted in 1999 and sentenced to 37 years in prison.

This case went so far as to have the Illinois governor pardon Anthony Porter.

Sometime after Porter was released, he then told a story about torture by police. He seemed bitter about his arrest and incarceration. He would eventually sue the state for compensation for his time spent in prison.

A federal inquiry was conducted regarding the allegations of abuse in the initial interview, and all the available witnesses were interviewed. When they interviewed Inez Jackson, whom they now knew was Simon's ex-wife, they found discrepancies in her account of the incident. The flaws in Inez Jackson's story were that if Inez was there, that would have made it two men and two women in the bleachers, and all the witnesses had seen three men and one woman. Inez also placed the time much earlier in the evening, and she had the number of shots different from the evidence from the autopsies.

When they interviewed Walter Jackson, they found out that Anthony Porter was incarcerated with Jackson, and Porter had convinced Jackson and Jackson's aunt to help him get out of prison by saying that he was working with Professor Protess and the professor would help them. Jackson later admitted he lied and had been convinced by Porter, who told him Professor Protess could get him out of prison.

The new investigation surmised that Anthony Porter, who was in prison, contrived the whole scheme using his friend Walter Jackson and Simon's ex-wife, along with the help of Protess and the student journalists.

None of the other witnesses said they saw Alstory Simon anywhere near the pool area that early morning. They said that it was Anthony Porter who was at the pool during the time of the murders.

After it finally broke that all those witnesses had lied, the only evidence remaining was Simon's confession.

Simon said it was a false confession. He said that he was intoxicated and felt threatened, and thought it was his only choice.

Afterward, the PI acknowledged that he had used a fake video to get Simon to confess, but said that he could use any method he wanted to get his job done.

Ironically, the PI's use of controversial methods to get the confession is a familiar chorus within the innocence community. They often argue that police should not use these same controversial methods to elicit confessions. There is even a category for it on the Exoneration Registry: Police Misconduct.

Simon also said that his attorney told him to confess and plead guilty to the crimes. Investigators later discovered that Simon's attorney was friends with and shared office space with Professor Protess and the PI who had taken his confession. This would seem to have been an apparent conflict of interest that an attorney with close contact to Protess was representing Simon.

In 2005, Simon's ex-wife, Inez Jackson, on her deathbed, recanted her statements that Simon had committed the crime. She admitted she was asked to lie to help Porter.

The media finally came around to the fact that Simon was railroaded by Protess and the students at the Northwestern journalism school in order to celebrate their freeing of Anthony Porter from death row. It seemed they had a vested interest in Anthony Porter and were wrapped up in the Innocence Machine.

Also in 2005, Porter filed a lawsuit against the state for compensation for his time spent in prison. All the police officers in the case were named in Porter's lawsuit. They were accused of railroading Porter and of other police misconduct. The assumption was that since he was deemed innocent by innocence advocates, he should be compensated for his time in prison.

In defending the lawsuit, the State reviewed the case and reinterviewed the witnesses who testified in the civil proceedings. The jury refused to award Porter any compensation and concluded that the police had probable cause to arrest Porter in the original case.

In addition to the Porter case, Professor Protess and his students were also accused of a number of journalistic improprieties in another case involving Anthony McKinney. In 2011, Professor Protess was suspended by the university for allegedly doctoring records. The university's attorneys resigned after initially representing the university in the case, but then suggested that Protess had lied to them and altered an archived email message. The university issued a statement that its professor had knowingly misrepresented the facts and his actions to the university, its attorneys, and the Medill dean on numerous documented occasions.

Protess has since been ousted from his position at Northwestern, ostensibly due to the controversy surrounding the Anthony McKinney innocence case. After that, the school dean presented a case against him, and he was told he would be let go. Protess then retired.

On October 22, 2013, the Cook County State's Attorney's Office announced that the murder case of Jerry Hillard and Marilyn Green would be reopened.

In October 2014, the office announced that the

charges against Simon had been vacated, after he served 15 years in prison. The State's Attorney announced in a press conference that the reinvestigation conducted by a journalist professor, a civilian private investigator, and young journalism students was flawed. The State's Attorney said that Protess and his team's investigation involved a series of alarming, coercive, and inappropriate tactics. When asked by a journalist at the press conference if Protess could be charged with any crime, the State's Attorney said that the statute of limitations had expired.

In an interesting twist of fate, some people believe in Professor Protess' innocence. They say he was innocent in the case brought forward by the university that resulted in his ousting from the Northwestern Medill Journalism School, and he was innocent in the information brought forward by the Cook County State's Attorney about his actions in the Porter and Simon cases.

In the end, it turns out that substantial evidence does show that Anthony Porter was guilty of the murders and that the evidence presented by Professor Protess' students was flawed and misguided.

Like almost everyone else in prison, Porter always claimed to be innocent. He made numerous appeals to be released before Protess, and his team contacted him.

Anthony Porter was not an innocent man in his life. He had a criminal record, which included violating probation by robbing and assaulting a victim; for that crime, he pleaded guilty to robbery and bail jumping and was sentenced to three years in prison. He was also arrested for theft and sentenced to one year in jail. Henry Williams said that Porter had robbed him at gunpoint just prior to the shootings. Earl Lewis testified that Porter shot and almost killed him in a dispute over Porter kicking his dog. Douglas McGhee testified that Porter had robbed him at gunpoint at one time at the exact location of the murders. Six people had identified him as having taken part in the murder of the two young people.

Why would anyone think that this man should be free and out in society? A defense attorney may say that even if a person is a criminal who has done heinous things in his past, it doesn't mean he is a monster and should be convicted for a crime he didn't commit. However, in this case, there is ample evidence that Porter did in fact commit this heinous, monstrous crime.

There is still a website dedicated to Anthony Porter's innocence, titled "Long Live Anthony Porter," which is hosted on the Chicago Torture Justice Center website.

This case should make everyone question the credibility of all innocence cases. Not only did the Protess team free an undoubtedly guilty man, but they also railroaded an innocent man into prison. That is not what an innocence project should do.

This case highlights what can happen when the quest to find an innocent person becomes all-consuming, causing those involved to become blind to other aspects. This results in the dismissal of incriminating evidence.

The Porter case is one in which an inmate essentially rules the asylum, or, in this case, the Innocence Machine.

This can also explain why, at times, innocent activists resort to securing the release of individuals on technicalities in a case. At least they're getting them released. Mission partly accomplished. But do they consider that they might have released a guilty person from prison?

CHAPTER 4
MAKING AN EXONEREE WEBSITE

Here is a program designed to help students become immersed in researching wrongful conviction cases.

From the Making an Exoneree website: "This is an extraordinary and unprecedented course and program. Every spring semester since 2018, a group of highly motivated Georgetown University undergraduate students has reinvestigated likely wrongful conviction cases, produced short documentaries that suggest innocence, and created social media campaigns calling for exonerations.

"This 5-credit course — formally labeled GOVX 400, Prison Reform Project, but informally known as "Making an Exoneree" — is unique in multiple respects. It is highly selective, with approximately 100 applicants for about 15 spaces, which are reserved for passionate and highly-motivated students. The class does not have readings, papers, or exams. Instead, the students spend an intensive semester as investigative journalists, documentarians, and social justice activists, with the goal of creating a public documentary (in addition to a website and social media campaign) that makes the case for the innocence of a wrongfully convicted person who is currently languishing in prison. Students leave campus regularly and travel to visit their "client" as they reinvestigate the crime and conviction. Their task is to portray the main issues, challenges, injustices, and human stories involved in each case.

"Making an Exoneree takes on difficult cases that are often overlooked by other innocence projects. These cases are often decades old without DNA evidence or available appeals. The students' ultimate goal is to breathe new life into these cases and help bring innocent people home from prison, utilizing every available resource and tailoring their approach to the specific case."

This appears to coincide with efforts to keep the Innocence Machine going strong.

CHAPTER 5
LEGAL STRATEGIES

Are attorneys snookered by the attractive allure of being able to stick it to the system and exonerate a convicted person? Is there a special *cachet* for attorneys who take high-profile cases, such as the Menendez brothers or Scott Peterson (both discussed later in this book), even though most true crime aficionados, having reviewed the evidence in these cases, and most law enforcement officials, believe they were appropriately convicted? Is there the attractive lure of being put in the spotlight as an exceptional attorney by getting someone acquitted after another (lesser) attorney failed?

Is there an allure for innocence program attorneys to find evidence that was never submitted for analysis, or to conduct new analyses, such as DNA testing? Even in cases with a substantial amount of other inculpatory evidence, what are the chances that DNA testing will provide a "Someone Else Did It" [SEDI] or "Some Other Dude Did It" [SODDI]) This captivating tactic has been known to backfire, as seen in the cases of David Temple, where the defense tried to blame the crime on a neighbor, and Kaitlyn Conley (both covered in more detail later in this book), who tried to blame her poison murder on her ex-boyfriend.

It is self-evident that wrongful convictions, although they do occur and are despicable, constitute a minuscule percentage of criminal convictions. Are there just as many backfires of wrongful conviction campaigns as wrongful convictions? No, that cannot be.

Or is there a similar number of convictions reversed solely due to technicalities? Even when the person, based on the original evidence, appears to be guilty?

Do attorneys and innocence advocates *intentionally overlook inculpatory evidence in their quest to prove* the innocence of a convicted person? Do innocence advocates create their podcasts or documentaries with the purposeful intention of presenting only evidence that raises questions about the innocence of their subject?

Do these podcasts or documentaries deliberately filter the evidence to make the story more compelling? Presenting the few instances of the crime that remain unanswered? (There are always unanswered questions.)

Does anybody wonder who really did it? Who else has as much inculpatory evidence, not just questions, as the person convicted?

Is the true crime public being duped by the media? By the Free My Guy or Gal websites, protests, and family campaigns? Are people conned into supporting a "wrongfully convicted" person by being presented with biased details?

Can podcasts and true crime documentaries manipulate judges and the public into believing a person is innocent? Even in the face of substantial inculpatory evidence?

Are innocence activists actually intellectually lazy, not doing the research on the case, and missing the real details of the incriminating evidence?

Are innocence advocates getting people to buy into the wrong narrative about the case?

Are those people who are concerned about the wrongfully convicted even slightly deterred by innocence campaigns that were eventually proven wrong?

Is there faux gravitas present in documentaries that profess the innocence of convicted people? Does it create a fake atmosphere of pretended seriousness and importance?

Is there a performative aspect for innocence campaign attorneys to achieve a result? Does it feed some attorneys' egos?

Should a convicted person be released due to police malfeasance, a technicality, prosecutorial misconduct, evidence mishandling, witness omissions, or even exculpatory evidence not presented?

Should a convicted person still be released if there is significant incriminating evidence? Should other inculpatory evidence be ignored due to these other factors?

Released to Kill Again

Perhaps an innocence project campaign is not directly responsible for a convict's release, but the general culture of innocence does influence this decision. This atmosphere will be featured in other cases. Unfortunately, this atmosphere of innocence has been around for a long time.

In April 1986, a young woman was driving to her gym when her Mustang broke down, and she pulled over on the side of Interstate 35 in Oklahoma. A man picked her up, promising to take her to a payphone. The man drove the woman to a nearby motel, tied her up, and assaulted her. When he allowed her to use the bathroom, she escaped and called the police.

The young woman was the daughter of a deputy sheriff, and she soon identified William Reece as her attacker. Reece was a truck driver and was subsequently located and arrested. He posted bail and was released.

About a month after his release, Reece assaulted another woman and was arrested. He was put on trial for both assaults, found guilty, and sentenced to 25 years in prison. Reece's attorneys appealed the conviction, and a court granted a review that found procedural errors in his case, resulting in a reduced sentence. He was paroled in 1996.

Reece then moved into his mother's home in Anadarko, Oklahoma. In 1997, he moved down to Houston, TX.

In the fall of 1997, 19-year-old Sandra Sapaugh stopped at a gas station in Webster, TX, to use a payphone. She discovered her tire had been slashed in a parking lot and drove to a Waffle House for help. A man came up to her, offering help, grabbed her, and forced her into his truck and drove out on the highway. Sapaugh jumped out of his speeding truck on the highway along I-45, severely injuring herself.

Sapaugh was taken to a hospital, and she described her attacker. Later, she was put under hypnosis, and she remembered the truck's license plate. The tag belonged to William Reece. Police presented her with a photo array, and Sapaugh picked out Reece. This information led to Reece's arrest and eventually his conviction in 1998. This time, he was sentenced to 60 years in prison.

In 2015, William Reece's DNA was matched to the murder of 19-year-old Tiffany Johnston. Johnston had been assaulted, beaten, and strangled. On September 21, 2015, Reece was charged with Johnston's murder.

In early 2016, Reece confessed to three more murders in Texas during 1997. He provided a map with other burial sites for his victims.

It should sound familiar that a convicted person's attorneys filed an appeal based upon prosecutorial misconduct, inadequate legal defense, official misconduct, or some other technicality, and the person duly convicted by a jury is released. Some individuals with extensive criminal records are released due to procedural errors or technicalities. Some will go on and commit further crimes. William Reece was released based on his attorney's appeals due to procedural errors. Reece went on to kill at least five more women before getting caught and ultimately being put in prison again.

Insufficient Evidence? Released To Commit Further Crimes

On September 12, 1989, Andrew Golden and his wife, Ardelle, returned home after a drive to Lake Hartridge in Winter Haven, FL. According to Andrew, Ardelle had lost her cigarette case, and she drove back to the lake to retrieve it. Andrew said he then went to bed.

The next morning, Andrew noticed that his wife had not returned and that her car was still gone. Golden called the police to report his wife missing.

Police found Ardelle's body in the lake, with her car near her body, also in the lake. An autopsy was conducted, and a medical examiner determined she had drowned.

Police interviewed Andrew Golden several times within the next couple months. They asked him if there was any insurance on her, and he initially denied having any policy on her life. However, at a later interview, he said he thought there might be one through her employer. Investigators eventually discovered that Golden had taken out a policy on his wife just two days before her drowning.

In time, Golden admitted that, while they were at the lake, they went for a swim. He said Ardelle was not a good swimmer, and that they came home that evening. He said that Ardelle went out to get a pack of cigarettes and returned to the lake to find her cigarette lighter from the dock where they had gone swimming.

When police looked in her purse, they discovered her glasses, a cigarette lighter, and a pack of cigarettes. Her car was found in the lake's shallow water. They also found that the depth of the water in the area where she drowned was only about three feet. When police looked into Golden's finances, they found he hadn't worked for two years and was about $250,000 in debt. They also discovered he had three more insurance policies on his wife taken out about four months before her death.

Golden was arrested in April 1990, and in October

1991, he was put on trial in Polk County, FL. On October 25, 1991, the jury convicted Andrew Golden of his wife's murder, and the jury voted to impose the death penalty.

Golden was in prison on death row; however, in November 1993, the Florida Supreme Court reversed the conviction and ordered the case dismissed for insufficient evidence. Andrew Golden was released in January 1994.

According to the National Registry of Exonerations, in 1999, Golden pled guilty in Dallas, TX, to three counts of taking indecent liberties with a child.

This case can be added to the list of exonerations or releases in which the convicted person was freed only to go on to commit further crimes.

CHAPTER 6
A MINEFIELD

International Wrongful Conviction Day is October 2.

PRESENTING THE MISTAKES OF INNOCENCE IN THE wake of the good work the innocence system does can be a minefield. However, some of these cases are difficult to ignore.

The typical strategy of the Innocence Machine is to recast the case in an emotional, compelling narrative for public consumption, altering the case away from the criminal violence and ignoring the facts. The Innocence Machine often cherry picks some details, leaving in a little bit of the truth, inserting them into the case narrative, diminishing them, like in the Adnan Syed case, discussed later in this book.

One should realize that the innocence movement is lawyer-based. It is from the perspective of attorneys, trial defense, and the appellate. This is not necessarily that of the general public, prosecutors, or forensic scientists. This is important to understand because defense attorneys are constantly seeking ways to win their cases. They are always looking for strategies to spin the narrative to convince a jury of a defendant's innocence. Defense attorneys are also usually anti law enforcement and anti forensic science because that is the bane of their existence; that is how they usually lose.

There appears to be no established policy or procedure for thoroughly vetting and investigating the innocence of individuals who have been convicted. Who is qualified to do the investigation? Are students, freshly minted lawyers, or interns qualified to conduct these investigations? Certainly not the students in the Anthony Porter case where they made so many false assumptions about the details of the crime.

Are seasoned academics even remotely qualified? For that matter, are appellate judges? Take cases where DNA isn't enough, like in the Patrick Willis case (discussed next), or where fingerprints aren't sufficient, as in the Melvin Mikes case (discussed later in this book).

This is part of the problem. Who is doing the investigation? Lawyers or academics? Who is better qualified, someone associated with law enforcement, a seasoned investigator, or an academic? Even an academic teaching forensic science? There is an academic in California who has built a career criticizing forensic science. Still, his degree was in history, science and technology studies, and European cultural studies. Does an academic have the qualifications to criticize forensic science or to develop an innocence case?

There are plenty of examples of academics writing articles about fingerprints that do not seem to know the first thing about fingerprints, such as their nature and uniqueness.

Is there an inherent arrogance in the academic world that can lead to these false assumptions? Is there an arrogance in the law school community? Is the combination of ego and arrogance leading to so many misfires of the Innocence Machine?

When innocence activists review the crime, they seem to be re-staging the crime scene to fit their idea that the person is innocent. The assessment of the crime scene, the language used to describe the incident, and the description of the defendant's morality do not always reflect the actual circumstances of the case.

It seems our society prefers to believe in the mythological Perry Mason and Ben Matlock defending their always innocent clients. Of course, people don't think *everyone* is innocent, but it seems that for every person convicted, there's someone who thinks they are innocent.

It appears that no matter how much cumulative incriminating evidence there is for a convicted murderer, there is always someone who thinks that person is innocent. That's the Innocence Machine. It also suggests that true crime enthusiasts and wannabe true crime investigators are scrutinizing every case with the possibility that the convicted person may be innocent.

The Innocence Machine can take almost any case and, with the right strategy, marketing, and lobbying, turn it into an innocence project. At least that is the impression when these cases are analyzed. Believe the convicted person, minimize incriminating evidence, and promote an innocence campaign.

The true crime obsession likely predated Ann Rule's books and the famous *Serial* podcast, and it appears to have a permanent place in media today. A logical offshoot of true crime is the innocence craze.

DNA Isn't Enough, Leads to Hung Jury

Sometimes, cases listed in the National Registry of Exonerations show that even a preponderance of DNA evidence was not enough to convince a jury of a defendant's guilt.

On January 31, 1992, Cheryl Walker was found dead by a small creek that ran through a neighborhood East of Oakland, CA. Walker was naked; she had been battered and had a rope around her neck. Her clothes were not found.

Neighbors reported hearing screaming in the creek area on January 28 and 29.

On February 11, the body of Marsha Gulley was found in the same neighborhood. Gulley had been stabbed 33 times, and her pants had been pulled down.

During the autopsies of the women, swabs were obtained from their bodies for later DNA analysis. An analysis of the material obtained from Gulley was conducted in 2000, and again in 2001. The criminalist in the second testing observed sperm, but stated that the sample was not sufficient for DNA testing.

The sample for the Walker autopsy was also analyzed in 2001 and then submitted into the FBI's Combined

DNA Index System (CODIS). In 2003, the system search returned a hit, and the DNA swab from Walker was confirmed as Patrick Willis' DNA. In 2006, genetic testing of material found under Cheryl Walker's fingernails also yielded a DNA match to Willis.

Patrick Willis was arrested in 2010 and charged with murder in Walker's death.

Astonishingly, the charge was dismissed by the Alameda County District Attorney for insufficient evidence.

In 2011, the Oakland police requested another analysis of the Marsha Gulley swabs. The lab technicians used equipment not available in 2000 or 2001 to recover sufficient DNA for testing. That testing included Willis as a potential contributor to the partial profile on Gulley's swab.

Police arrested Willis in December 2012, and he was charged with two counts of murder. Patrick Willis' trial was held in Alameda County Superior Court in July 2013. Along with the forensic DNA evidence, the state showed that Willis' mother lived near where both victims were found.

Eventually, Willis admitted that he'd had sexual contact with both women, who were sex workers, which would explain the DNA evidence. He denied, however, that he killed either one.

On July 22, 2013, a jury convicted Willis of two counts of first-degree murder, and he was later sentenced to life in prison without parole.

Willis' attorneys appealed his conviction, and California's First District Court of Appeal reversed and granted him a new trial on April 29, 2019, citing inadequate defense.

In this new trial in 2019, the defense presented the argument that "Just because he had sexual interaction with both of these women, that doesn't make him a killer…"

On May 5, 2021, the jury told the judge they could not reach a verdict, and a mistrial was declared. Willis was released on May 11. After this mistrial, the prosecution decided to dismiss the charges. Willis sued the state of California and was awarded $441,842 in compensation.

The suggestion of a coincidence of Willis just having consensual sexual relations with two women who were murdered just after he visited them is staggering. It seems that the defense here was SOSDI: Some other sucker did it.

Observe the language of the entry in the National Registry of Exonerations: "With regards to the Walker sample, testing was completed in 2001 but not submitted to the FBI's Combined DNA Index System, known as CODIS, for two more years. In 2003, the FBI said 39-year-old Patrick Willis' genetic profile was consistent with a partial profile found on Walker's oral swab. In 2006, the police asked for testing of genetic material found under Walker's fingernails. That testing didn't occur until 2009, and those results also said the material was consistent with Willis' genetic profile."

This is a DNA match, pure and simple. However, the language of "consistent with a partial profile" is highly misleading. In the second DNA match, "results said that the material was consistent with Willis' genetic profile" is also misleading, as this was a second DNA match to the defendant. Patrick Willis' DNA was inside the victim's body. This is straightforward and uncomplicated, and does not coincide with any watering down of the terms.

Perhaps this is the language the defense used in the trial, which could explain why the jury was unable to reach a verdict in this case.

CHAPTER 7

EVIDENCE SHOULD DECIDE — NOT NARRATIVE

One thing that frequently comes up when people are looking to exonerate a defendant is that they do not recognize or accept the direct evidence or a "smoking gun" proving his guilt; therefore, he must be innocent. The problem with this thinking is that there is rarely a smoking gun in criminal trials, especially murder trials. If a person is well aware of evidence from all the CSI shows, they may believe they can commit the perfect crime and not leave evidence. While it may be sparse, likely there will be some type of evidence left behind.

Human beings don't like complex situations without clear-cut answers. They want cases to be black-and-white, distinct, crystal-clear, with no room for ambiguity: innocent or guilty. Crime is often the result of multiple, complex, and interrelated factors, and many facts cannot be established or verified with certainty. There may not be smoking gun evidence to rely on.

If there is no smoking gun evidence or direct evidence, then the case will almost always be circumstantial.

Circumstantial does not mean innocent. An accumulation of circumstantial evidence also points to guilt. With circumstantial evidence, nearly everything, all the conditional circumstances accumulated, can also lead to the guilt of a person.

It seems that the Innocence Machine tells everyone to ignore multiple pieces of incriminating evidence, like DNA, suggesting all of it was conspiratorially planted by the biased police.

A case in review should be examined based on the evidence, ignoring all the noise of the activists and the media, and concentrating strictly on the evidence.

CHAPTER 8

DESENSITIZATION AND EMOTION

One consequence of the Innocence Machine is the desensitization of the horrible crimes some of these people have committed, and the dismissal of the victims of these crimes. Even in cases of actual innocence, verified by DNA, the emphasis is on the wrongly convicted and not on the victims.

Emotion is a grand factor in the Innocence Machine. It is often the intensity of a crime and the perceived horrors of prison that suck people in. It is a normal human emotion that people care about and can have empathy for someone in the terrible position of being in prison for a crime that they did not commit — and the concept that, under the right circumstances, almost anyone could end up like that, too.

Those with an ethical and moralistic approach may base this on a desire to instill some normality into a system that seems chaotic. However, innocence activists often have to engage in mental contortions to shape the circumstances and conclude that these people might be innocent.

There can be a cognitive dissonance between the actual evidence and the evidence that may point to innocence. Innocence advocates may ignore evidence that points to guilt and overemphasize situations that they believe points to innocence.

At times, innocence activists lose themselves in the details and spin elaborate theories of the situation, merged with a complex narrative that fits what they want to believe while rejecting a rational view of all the facts of the case.

Sometimes, people claiming a defendant's innocence or innocence advocates ask the public or audience to engage in mental gymnastics to convince us of their subject's innocence. Leading the scenario toward innocence, but like playing Twister, switching and baiting specific case facts. Like the bizarre story about a burglary turned into kidnapping, turned into murder, and, the murderers following the news, placing the body in San Francisco Bay, to frame the defendant, Scott Peterson. Or a kidnapper turned murderer writing an excessively long note, placing a self-made fake garotte on the body, and leaving by a high window instead of the front door (among other things) after killing Jon Benet Ramsey.

The Innocence Machine smacks of a game. Let's find a convicted criminal with something unusual in their case and discover the one thing that shows they might be innocent. In real life, few crimes are as perfect as what one might see on TV. It is rare to have everything answered, and in reality, all evidence, timelines, and motives are not always neatly wrapped up, especially if the person was trying not to get caught, if the crime was preplanned, or if the perpetrator has committed the crime before and is good at it. Often, the only people who know what really happened are the perpetrator and the victim.

No innocent person should remain in prison; however, it seems the Innocence Machine creates an environment where advocating for someone they believe is innocent becomes a noble quest, worthy of admiration and approbation.

As components of the machine, hundreds of websites, slogans, signs, and T-shirts promote the innocence of an accused or convicted person. There is even a movement to crowdsource cold cases.

Guilty or not guilty, some recent documentaries and podcasts have exploited this innocence craze, presenting the case in a narrow way to create emotion and excitement. This makes for compelling, "page-turning" viewing and listening, but not necessarily for getting at the truth.

Some of these podcasts and TV shows suggest there is always police corruption, cover-ups, or mishandling of most cases. In reality, the perpetrators think they have the cunning to cover their tracks, bamboozle detectives, and convince their family and anyone who listens that they are innocent.

It should always be self-evident that a family might support their relatives. There will always be someone who believes that the accused is blameless. A possible example is the Gabby Petito case, where Brian Laundrie, based on his suicide note, admitted to the murder of Petito. Still, Laundrie's parents supported him and even had a lawyer waiting when he returned to Florida. (Since Laundrie committed suicide before he could be caught, let alone convicted, that case is not covered in this book.)

Innocence activists' podcasts and documentaries have tremendous power to change people's minds. Whether the purpose is to create a following or controversy, they can be very successful. Some of them can be compared to horror movies because their goal is to create emotion.

There is a maxim within the justice system that states that every convicted person claims to be innocent. Ellary A. Kane, forensic psychologist and author, says, "Prisons are filled with 'innocent' men: those who tell me, and anyone else who will listen, they're innocent, despite a mountain of evidence proclaiming otherwise, and those who actually are *innocent.* According to the Innocence Project, a litigation and public policy organization dedicated to exonerating wrongfully convicted individuals, between two and five percent of all prisoners in the United States are innocent of the crime for which they have been convicted. That means a portion of those 'innocent' men are telling the truth.

"In my work as a forensic psychologist, assertions of innocence are commonplace. My job affords a unique perspective, as many of the inmates I evaluate have been incarcerated for twenty or more years. *It is a relatively frequent occurrence to review a case in which an inmate professed his innocence for many years, only to eventually reveal his guilt.* Because I have encountered a substantial number of these types of cases, I know all too well that an 'innocent' man can easily turn into a guilty one."

The Innocence System has presented various statistics regarding the percentage of people who were wrongfully convicted. With the number of misfires uncovered, one wonders what the percentage of wrongly exonerated is among those listed as exonerations.

The question has to be asked: Do the ends justify the means? If it is wrong for the government to misrepresent itself and engage in misconduct, is it okay for the Innocence Machine? Are ethical causes pursued by unethical means appropriate? The Porter case comes to mind again.

Abuses within the Innocence Machine suggest that the justice system is open to manipulation by those seeking notoriety or some other reward.

CHAPTER 9

ORIGINS OF THE INNOCENCE PROJECT

The Innocence Project was founded in 1992 by attorneys Barry Scheck and Peter Neufeld. The organization centered on the power of DNA testing to be utilized in wrongful convictions. Scheck and Neufeld were both part of the team of lawyers that defended O. J. Simpson. The project became an independent nonprofit organization in 2003.

The Innocence Project is a wholly commendable endeavor to investigate and, hopefully, exonerate individuals within the justice system who are actually innocent. The effort to release a wrongly convicted person is certainly virtuous.

The Innocence Project website lists that, after it originated, "soon, a small group of lawyers, students, and volunteers took on cases to free wrongfully convicted people through DNA testing at the Benjamin N. Cardozo School of Law" in New York.

The Innocence Project goes on to list the many exonerations it has achieved from 1992 to the present. It has successfully overturned more than 300 convictions through DNA-based exonerations. These include several exonerations of persons on death row. The Innocence Project has worked on cases involving convictions throughout the United States and is part of the Innocence Network, which connects a wide range of innocence organizations. According to the National Registry of Exonerations, the Innocence Project has served as a model for many other innocence organizations across the U.S., resulting in over 3,000 exonerations.

In a bit of historical irony, in the O. J. Simpson case (discussed more later), Barry Scheck faced a prosecution with the most inculpatory or damning evidence in the history of jurisprudence, and successfully challenged the DNA and blood evidence provided. including DNA from both victims found in Simpson's bathroom and bedroom, and Simpson's DNA at the crime scene. It appears that Scheck suggests that DNA evidence could be contaminated, with a significant likelihood of false positives.

Since the O. J. case had so much incriminating evidence and O. J. was adjudicated responsible for the murders in a civil trial, the irony is that Scheck and Neufeld helped get a guilty man to be declared innocent and are now trying to get the release of convicted people whom they deem are innocent.

The Innocence Project and other innocence organizations are truly laudable and praiseworthy for their work in exonerating innocent people.

Deflection by Shaken Baby Syndrome

This case was presented by the Innocence Machine as one of a conviction based upon a debunked theory of "shaken baby syndrome," and that the defendant had autism. A magazine headline in September 2024 stated, "Texas is About to 'Execute Forrest Gump,' Lawyer warns."

In October 2024, the Office of the Attorney General released a statement titled, Office of the Attorney General Sets the Record Straight About Nikki Curtis' Death, Rebutting Jeff Leach's and Joe Moody's Lies About Convicted Child Murderer." The Attorney General stated that the activists were interfering with the justice system.

The case began when a two-year-old child was brought into the emergency room with extensive injuries all over her body. The child's father said that the injuries occurred when she fell from her bed.

The ER nurse would later testify that she saw what appeared to be a handprint on the child's face and that the back of the child's skull was bruised and what she described as "mushy." The nurse did not believe the extensive injuries resulted from a fall and immediately called the police.

Testimony during the trial from the family was that Roberson had a history of violence toward his daughter, and the family was afraid to leave him alone with her. Roberson's own mother said that "one of these days he's going to kill her and it's going to be too late for anyone to do anything about it."

Multiple physicians testified at the trial that the young child died from substantial blunt force injuries that indicated evidence of being struck. The extent of the injuries precluded the possibility that the child had been shaken.

The medical examiner (ME) who conducted the autopsy testified that she concluded that the child had been repeatedly struck, leaving clear impact wounds totally incompatible with being shaken. The ME noted a large subdural hematoma and brain swelling that was so severe that the brain had shifted in the child's head. These were deemed so acute that no single accident could have caused them. There was also evidence that the child's jaw had been shifted, possibly leading to pressure on the brain. These autopsy findings were later reviewed by six other medical examiners at the Dallas County Medical Examiner's office.

During interviews with Roberson, he repeatedly lied about how the incident happened, changing his story multiple times. He told different stories to the nurses at the hospital. When interviewed by the police, he said that his child had fallen out of bed. When questioned about the multiple injuries, he told police that she was clumsy and often fell down.

Roberson also told his girlfriend a story that the child had fallen on a brick floor. (The floor was carpeted.) The girlfriend testified that Roberson said to her "that if he did do it, he doesn't remember, that he snapped, and he doesn't remember doing it."

During the trial, other witnesses testified that Roberson had more than 12 prior arrests, including severe physical abuse of his ex-wife.

The Attorney General (AG) also indicated in his statement that "the jury did not convict Roberson on the basis of 'Shaken Baby Syndrome.' The 'junk science' objection that has been used as a pretext to interfere with the proceedings has no basis in reality."

In a press release, the AG also listed links to the original autopsy report and the original medical examiner's response to the innocence claims. Also listed were links to exhibits from the trial.

The Robert Roberson case displays the full force of the Innocence Machine. Innocence activists employed the strategy of distraction and utilized emotional appeals to create their narrative. By declaring that Roberson was convicted on the "debunked" theory of shaken baby syndrome, they most likely knew that this would be a trigger phrase that would suck in people emotionally. It became known that Roberson had autism, and knowing that there was currently great public awareness of this condition, this release was made in an attempt to be a mitigating factor. The comparison to Forrest Gump was surely designed to elicit an emotional response.

However, a thorough and careful examination of the trial transcripts and the AG's response reveals that Robert Roberson was rightly convicted of this heinous crime. His criminal history, the statements from the family about his violence, even his own mother's statements, and all the medical testimony provide a complete case for Roberson's guilt.

Linked to a Handgun and a Dagger

On October 18, 2005, Norma and Dennis Woodruff were found murdered in the living room of their own home.

Dennis was shot once and stabbed nine times, and his wife, Norma, had multiple gunshot wounds and was stabbed in the neck.

Texas Ranger Jeffery Collins' affidavit said, "There was no forced entry into the locked home. Valuables were left in plain sight, and a blood trail indicated that the killer washed up in a bathroom before leaving," according to an article in the *Royce City Herald-Banner.*

Police discovered that two days prior, their son, Brandon Woodruff, 19, had visited his parents. He told police he had a family dinner on Sunday and then left for their other nearby property. The local medical examiner was not able to precisely determine the time of death; it appeared they were attacked sometime between 9 p.m. and 11 p.m. that Sunday.

The investigation found that Norma had a phone conversation with her mother around 9 p.m., and the couple's daughter, Charla Woodruff, a college student in Arkansas, called around 11 p.m., but there was no answer.

The son, Brandon Woodruff, was further questioned about his whereabouts on that Sunday night, and police noted inconsistencies in his account of the timeline. During an interview with investigators, Brandon Woodruff said he was driving the Chevrolet pickup that night, although witnesses repeatedly testified that Norma Woodruff didn't let her son use the truck.

Within a short time after the murders, the mother of Brandon's girlfriend, Michelle Lee, contacted police to report that a gun and bullets were missing from her home. The weapon was a .45 caliber Long Colt handgun. She also relayed that Brandon had been in the Lees' home the weekend of the murders. Police responded to the home and recovered a .45 bullet that was kept near the missing gun. This bullet would later be compared to a bullet from the crime scene, and experts found they were consistent.

Another issue brought out during the investigation was that Brandon had been known to visit gay male clubs. They found several pictures of Brandon at these clubs.

Police further discovered during the investigation that Norma and Dennis, Brandon's parents, had mentioned to a relative that they were going to confront Brandon about his failing at college and his sexuality at that Sunday dinner.

The investigation into the murders continued, and in June 2008, a family member found a dagger in the barn of the Woodruff's old house in Heath, TX. This was the location Brandon had told the police he went to after the Sunday dinner with his parents. After laboratory analysis, Dennis Woodruff's blood was found on this weapon. Brandon Woodruff's former college roommate stated that the dagger was the same one Woodruff had in his dorm room. The medical examiner could definitively say that the dagger was the weapon used in the attacks.

Police received information that a neighbor observed Brandon Woodruff arrive at the Heath residence at around 11 p.m. on October 16. The neighbor also noted that the next morning, the vehicle Brandon had been driving was parked at the home, and the pickup truck belonging to the couple who lived there was gone.

During the subsequent questioning of Brandon, police noticed he kept changing his story about the times he was to pick up his friend for travel back to his university, as well as information about the dagger found at the house he was at that evening, the possible identification of him and his truck at the scene of the crime, and the theft of a gun very similar to the type of weapon used in the crime that was found to be missing soon after Brandon visited his girlfriend's home.

Brandon Woodruff was arrested in October 2005, and his trial began in 2009. During the trial, Brandon's friends testified that he was supposed to pick them up at 5 p.m. in Dallas the day of the murder for a ride to Abilene Christian University. But Brandon had called them to change the time and place. Another friend testified he believed Woodruff would pick him up at home in Denton that evening for the ride back to college. Instead, he met up with Woodruff at a Dallas restaurant several hours later.

A neighbor of the Woodruffs in Heath testified he observed Brandon Woodruff at the Heath residence shortly after 10 p.m. on October 16, 2005, and that Norma Woodruff's Chevrolet pickup, which had been parked at the Heath residence, was gone the next morning. Brandon Woodruff's older Dodge pickup was parked in its place.

Charla Woodruff, the defendant's sister and, at the time of the trial, a Miller County Sheriff's Department investigator, testified for the prosecution that she had tried to call her mother at about 11 p.m. on the Sunday of the murders. Charla said she asked Woodruff what time he had left the Royse City home, and he told her he had left at 6:30 p.m. to give a friend a ride back home to Abilene Christian University.

Additionally, evidence was presented to the court

about the condition of the crime scene, the weapon missing from Brandon's girlfriend's house, the dagger, Dennis Woodruff's blood on the dagger found in the other house where Brandon was staying, the discrepancies in Brandon's answers to time frame questions, and his whereabouts and the vehicles.

The jury found him guilty of the murder of his parents in October 2009, and he was sentenced to life in prison without parole.

In a 2018 book, *Railroaded: The Homophobic Prosecution of Brandon Woodruff for His Parents' Murders*, Phillip Crawford, Jr. suggested that the investigation and conviction were homophobic and unjust. Woodruff supporters, sometimes protesting with signs, placards, and the website freebrandon.org, claimed that Brandon being gay was a major factor in the jury's guilty verdict.

Text from the Innocence Project Texas website: "In 2009, Brandon's case went to trial in Hunt County, a rural area in East Texas. Throughout the trial, the fact that Brandon was gay was consistently stated by the prosecution, who used his sexuality as an implication of his character; a bias that impacted both the investigation and the trial, as several jurors described homosexuality as immoral during the voir dire process. Despite a lack of physical evidence, eyewitnesses, an exact time of death, and missing murder weapons, Brandon was found guilty of capital murder and sentenced to life in prison. IPTX continues to work toward Brandon's exoneration."

Since Brandon Woodruff has been sent to prison, the Innocence Project of Texas has taken up his case. The main objection the people at the Texas Innocence Project have with the conviction in the Woodruff case is the timeline. They say he would have had only 19 minutes to commit the crime, which was not enough time to do all that was done in that time frame. They also mentioned that because Brandon was so calm on the phone, in what would have been right after the murders, he couldn't have done it.

As reconstructed by the prosecution, the timeline is only restricted by the supporters of innocence. The available time would certainly not make it impossible, even if it were very small. Additionally, someone's demeanor after a heinous crime is not really a gauge of their prior actions.

Brandon Woodruff was granted a new trial in 2009, primarily based on the work of the Texas Innocence Project. According to their website, the new trial was punctuated by implications of Brandon's sexuality as background for his crimes. The website also highlights the absence of the gun, the time frame for the murder, and the lack of an exact time of death.

All this in the face of every piece of evidence pointing directly toward the defendant.

During the trial, held in Hunt County, East Texas, the prosecution presented all of the same evidence as the first trial, and Brandon Woodruff was again convicted of capital murder and sentenced to life in prison.

The Brandon Woodruff case is a prime example of individuals within the innocence movement disregarding substantial incriminating evidence and focusing on a narrow aspect of the case. In this instance, the narrow aspect is not exculpatory; it is just questionable. The supporters of Brandon Woodruff do not normally address the damning and inculpatory evidence on the websites and responses to his conviction, seeming to ignore that the victim's DNA was found on a dagger that was located at a home where Brandon was staying, the weapon missing from his girlfriend's house, and the other evidence presented.

CHAPTER 10

INNOCENCE PROJECT SUCCESS STORIES

The Innocence Project website text says, "In the last 30 years, exoneration cases have exposed the very real short-comings of the American legal system."

CENTRAL PARK 5: A LEGITIMATE CASE

A well-publicized wrongful conviction case is known as the Central Park Five case. This resulted in the wrongful convictions of five young men for the attack and assault of a young woman, Trisha Meili, who was jogging in New York City's Central Park on April 19, 1989.

This was a high-profile case with a media frenzy about the circumstances of the assault. The police arrested five young men and charged them with the crime, but they did not have a lot of evidence connecting the men to the crime. Most of the men confessed during the police interviews. One young man later said his father told him to confess so that the police could help him. Based upon their confessions, the five men were tried and convicted and spent several years in prison. Eventually, they were exonerated after someone else confessed to the crimes.

In 2002, a man already in prison for attacking five women and known as a serial rapist, Matias Reyes, confessed to the assault of Trisha Meili and said he was the only person present during the crime. A DNA comparison confirmed his guilt.

Subsequently, the convictions of the five men in the case were vacated in 2002. This is a legitimate success for the activists for wrongful conviction.

KIMBERLY LONG: A LEGITIMATE CASE

In the early morning of October 6, 2003, Kimberly Long arrived at her Corona, CA, home and discovered her boyfriend, Ozzy Conde, murdered. Conde had been bludgeoned to death in the living room of the home they shared, and some items were placed that appeared to have been collected for theft. She immediately called 911. The police suspected she was the culprit, but Long denied being involved.

A witness came forward who identified Long as being at the scene. The witness stated he had dropped her off at approximately 1:20 a.m., which would have placed her there just before the 911 call. Witnesses said they heard the couple arguing that evening.

Kimberly Long was arrested, and the case went to trial in February 2005 in Riverside County, CA. A mistrial was declared when the jury could not reach a unanimous verdict. In December 2005, Long went to trial a second time and was convicted this time and sentenced to 15 years to life in prison.

The California Innocence Project took up the case and, based on forensic pathology evidence that put the victim's time of death much earlier in the evening and the presence of unknown male DNA on some items that were positioned to be stolen, in November 2020, the California Supreme Court unanimously overturned Kimberly's murder conviction. In April 2021, all charges were formally dismissed, resulting in Kimberly's full exoneration.

CHAPTER 11

SEMINAL INNOCENCE ADVOCATES: A FILM & A PODCAST

The Thin Blue Line

A seminal true crime documentary about the innocence of the convicted was presented in the movie by Errol Morris, *The Thin Blue Line*. Released in 1988, the documentary centered on the trial and conviction of Randall Dale Adams for the 1976 shooting of a Dallas police officer. The film revealed inconsistencies in the original case and elicited an admission from an original suspect, David Harris.

The film, which won numerous awards, was controversial at the time due to its use of reenactments, in which actors recreated the crime. Though it is now an accepted and universal documentary technique, this was possibly the first time it was used in a true crime documentary. During closing arguments in Adam's trial, the prosecutor used the phrase that the police are the "thin blue line" protecting society from crime and chaos.

Possibly due to the documentary, Randall Adams'

conviction was overturned by the Texas Court of Criminal Appeals. Prosecutors declined to retry Adams, who had spent 12 years in prison, for the crime.

A Plethora of Incriminating Evidence

Hae Min Lee was last seen at about 3 p.m. on January 13, 1999, driving a gray 1998 Nissan Sentra. Her body was discovered in a shallow grave in Baltimore's Leakin Park on February 9. An autopsy revealed she had been killed by manual strangulation. On February 12, police received a phone call that suggested they look at Lee's ex-boyfriend, Adnan Syed. After an investigation, Syed was arrested on February 28 and charged with first-degree murder.

During the trial, prosecutors presented voluminous inculpatory and damming evidence. Syed's fingerprints were found on a piece of "floral paper" (presumably the type of paper used to wrap flowers) in the trunk of Hae's car. Adnan's left palm print was found on the back cover of a map book of the Baltimore area, with the page showing Leakin Park torn out and missing.

Most significant was Jay Wilds' testimony, a friend of Syed's. Wilds testified that Syed had expressed intentions to kill Lee and stated that he had helped Syed bury Lee's body after Syed confessed to killing her on January 13. Wilds testified that Syed borrowed Wilds' car, and when he returned it, he had Lee's body in the trunk and asked for help. Wilds accurately identified the clothes Hae had been wearing when she left school that day. The significance was that Wilds was not a student and would not have otherwise known what she was wearing. Wilds also knew the location of Hae's car before it was found. All of this evidence is significant and cannot be dismissed as the testimony of an implausible witness.

Jay Wild's friend, Jennifer Pusateri, testified that Wild had told her he had been with Syed to dispose of Hae's body and that he told her Hae had been strangled, a fact that police had kept from the media. Pusateri also said that she and Wilds had disposed of a shovel in a dumpster behind a local mall. Pusateri said Wilds had told her about seeing Hae's body and that Syed had confessed to him that he had killed Hae Lee.

Additionally, a red fiber was found in Hae's hair that was consistent with Wild's contention that Syed had used red gloves when burying Hae in Leakin Park.

Testimony was also presented about Syed's cell phone records, and prosecutors used cell phone tower records to track Syed's whereabouts to back up Wilds' testimony. Syed's cell phone pinged at a cell tower antenna near Leakin Park on January 13. Phone records put Syed's phone near both the location of the body and the location of Hae's car. Furthermore, cell phone communication was also used to place Syed off campus during the critical hours on January 13. This testimony directly conflicted with Syed's statement about his whereabouts that day. In fact, Syed never presented an indisputable alibi for his time.

Additional testimony from other witnesses was also provided. A school nurse asserted that Syed had told her that on February 11, Hae had called him to say she wanted to get back together. This disputed Hae's diary entry that she had moved on from Syed and had a new boyfriend, adding to the apparent lies Syed had told during the investigation.

A friend of both Syed and Hae Lee, Krista Meyers, testified she had heard Adnan Syed ask Hae Lee for a ride after school that January morning. Krista said that Adnan said he needed a ride because his car was being repaired. Adnan's car never needed repair during that time frame.

When Hae was still missing, her father, Young Lee, found a number in Hae's diary next to her writing professing her love for her boyfriend, and Young called that number. Adnan answered the call and told Mr. Lee that Hae was going to give him a ride home from school. However, Adnan said he got detained, and Hae probably got tired of waiting for him and left.

Another interesting note from the cell phone call logs was that after January 13, Syed never tried to call Hae again. Hae's other friends tried to contact her after she was reported missing.

All this cumulative evidence reinforces the guilty verdict for Adnan Syed and his sentence of life in prison. (Note: On March 6, 2025, a Maryland judge granted Syed a sentence reduction to time served after spending 25 years in prison.)

SERIAL PODCAST

The formative podcast for activists of innocence is *Serial*, hosted by Sarah Koenig, which started in 2014 as an offshoot of the groundbreaking podcast *This American Life*. *Serial* examined the 1999 murder of Hae Min Lee, an 18-year-old high school student in Baltimore County,

Maryland, and convincingly advocated for the innocence of Adnan Syed, who was convicted of Lee's murder in 2000. Syed's first trial ended in a mistrial after jurors overheard a sidebar discussion between the judge and the defense. After a six-week second trial, Syed was found guilty of Lee's murder on February 25, 2000, and was given a life sentence.

The *Serial* podcast sparked several "Free Adnan" campaigns and the HBO docuseries *The Case Against Adnan Syed*, and set the standard for the true-crime podcasting craze.

Here is a quote from an analysis of the Adnan Syed case: "Out of all of the witnesses and all of the facts, the only hard evidence the prosecution had was Jay Wilds' testimony and Adnan's own cell phone records. Biased eyewitness testimony: The prosecution relied on the testimony of Jay Wilds, Adnan's acquaintance, who claimed that Adnan had confessed to him and involved him in the crime. Despite inconsistencies and changes in his story over time, the prosecution spun this testimony to present Jay as a credible witness. May 6, 2023."

There were no inconsistencies in Wild's testimony; there were discrepancies between what Syed said and Wilds statements. Other witnesses and cell phone tracking corroborated almost all of Wild's testimony, including Wild's description of the clothing the victim was wearing and the location of the victim's car. The case against Syed was substantial, even beyond Wild's testimony, with corroboration from a teacher, Wild's girlfriend, and others. There is no valid reason to ignore Wild's testimony in this case.

The innocence advocates in the Lee murder case cited the existence of a couple other possible suspects that the police had developed but did not turn over to the defense. On September 19, 2022, a judge, citing the prosecution's failure to hand over potentially beneficial evidence to the defense, overturned the conviction. This led to Syed being set free after 23 years in prison. The judge reinstated the murder conviction in March 2025, but reduced Syed's sentence to time served.

In 2023, an article was published at Quillette.com entitled *The Wrongful Exoneration of Adnan Syed Part I: A Straightforward Murder Case.* In it, Andrew Hammel listed all the trial evidence and wrote, "Adnan Syed would never have been released had *Serial* not been made. Advocacy journalism must be treated with caution." Society needs to stop musing that alternate suspects, alternate theories about the crime, issues that don't exactly match up, like time frames, and even alternative evidence, automatically make a defendant innocent. They do not.

Lee's murder was not the case of just one, possibly mistaken, witness, for whom there was no further evidence when discounted. There was substantial evidence that corroborated the testimony of numerous witnesses in the case. The evidence presented by Wilds, along with others' verification of his statements, was strongly incriminating.

Despite an impressive podcast that makes a compelling case for Syed's innocence, a careful, unbiased analysis reveals significant evidence that convincingly points to Adnan Syed's guilt. Enough to dispel any possibility of innocence.

CHAPTER 12

COMMON REASONS FOR INNOCENCE PROMOTED BY ACTIVISTS

Here are some common reasons activists use to proclaim a person's innocence:

Alternative Suspect

Many innocence activist websites state that one reason for an innocence claim is that there were other suspects possible in the case, and the police either didn't pursue them or didn't thoroughly investigate them. It should be evident that another suspect in the case does not mean the defendant is innocent.

The raising of alternative suspect(s) does not make someone innocent. It may be enough for a jury to acquit that person and raise some reasonable doubt, but it will not make the person innocent. Because another person was not thoroughly investigated (they probably were) does not make the person accused innocent. Sometimes, this tactic backfires, as in the case of the other possible suspect (OPS) in the David Temple case (discussed later), where the OPS testified, and the new witness was discredited. The possible other suspect testified that he did not commit the crime and a new witness said the OPS killed the dog at the crime scene, however, the dog was still alive.

Appearance

She is a sweet, dowdy-looking person; she does not look like someone who could have committed this horrible crime. He is a well-dressed, handsome young man and could never have committed such a gruesome act. Of course, appearance has no bearing on what a person has done in the world of crime.

Personality

Innocence advocates and defense attorneys will profess that just because they are horrible people, thieves, adulterers, or abusers, it doesn't make them guilty. They will declare that just because several coincidences or circumstances may point in their direction, it doesn't make them guilty. However, a person's personality, discretion, aggressiveness, and morality should be taken into account when evaluating their motives and ability to commit the action.

Often, the background of the case, the evidence, and the testimony all seem to fade into the background, with the personality of the convicted person taking center stage, and used to declare their innocence. An example of this is the Steven Avery case. Avery has a personable, confident, believable personality, but the vast deluge of incriminating evidence belies his personality.

Always Maintained Their Innocence

It is a common mantra on innocence organization websites that the convicted person has *always maintained their innocence.* Almost every person involved in the justice system, from prison wardens to prosecutors to forensic psychologists to defense attorneys, will state that nearly every convicted person has always maintained their innocence.

A Broken Justice System

A significant reason for the existence of innocence campaigns is that the current justice system is questionable and even broken.

An innocence organization serves an important purpose. This is evidenced by the exoneration of many convicted people through DNA testing, a reliable and unquestionable method, including a laudable 25 persons from death row.

However, there should be a question about appellate attorneys who clog up the system by filing redundant or frivolous appeals and motions. While it is recognized that any accused person or defendant should have all protections provided, appeals based on evidence that was improperly tested, victims of police misconduct (tunnel vision), ineffective trial counsel, and improper statements during the trial often seem peripheral when compared to inculpatory evidence presented during the trial.

Is there also an imbalance between the rights of the

suspect/convicted and those of the victims, families of the victims, and their right to justice?

Sometimes an appeal may be based on someone else's DNA found at the scene or even on the murder weapon. The implication is that there is an alternate suspect. However, this does not mean that the defendant is innocent. It can merely show that, at some point, someone else touched that item or was at that location.

Reasonable Doubt

Somehow, statements about reasonable doubt, the prosecution's failure to make its case, the lack of direct evidence, and a purely circumstantial case, as interpreted by innocence activists, all lead to an inference of innocence. They unequivocally do not. Reasonable doubt is a very subjective concept, and in almost every trial, the defense attorney will mention that phrase, "reasonable doubt." There is rarely direct evidence in criminal cases. When criminals are experienced and practiced, or when they are careful, there is not usually what most people would categorize as direct evidence, such as fingerprints or DNA. Unfortunately, there is often only circumstantial evidence in almost every crime, especially when the perpetrator is trying to avoid detection. The case comprises circumstances that lead to one suspect or the other.

Defense attorneys can interpret reasonable doubt very narrowly to try to restrict and confine a jury's thinking. An exact definition of reasonable doubt is difficult, and it can become easy for fair-minded jurors to become confused. It can also become a reason to vote not guilty.

Direct Evidence

There seems to be a pervasive lawyer axiom: If there is no direct evidence, the case is circumstantial and points to their client's innocence.

Circumstantial evidence can be damning and result in a case beyond a reasonable doubt. All the circumstances are compiled into an incriminating case.

A lawyer's thought is that without the smoking gun, which is usually considered DNA or an eyewitness, the defendant is innocent.

It is a myth that direct evidence is needed to convict someone beyond a reasonable doubt. Circumstantial evidence that links many pieces of evidence together to point to the defendant is very damning.

Bias

Defense attorneys will often present a case in which the police exhibited a bias, such as confirmation bias, in their handling of an investigation. That they already had their suspect and used the evidence to confirm their belief that that person was guilty.

Is there a reverse confirmation bias going on in the innocence movement? Do they have an automatically innocent bias? Where does the evidence mechanically confirm the innocence conclusion? And then where are the circumstances of innocence built around that assumption?

Poor Police Investigation

Sloppy investigations, often the standard argument of many defense attorneys, do not mean that the defendant is innocent. No matter how messed up an investigation or how bad the crime scene search was, the conclusion should not be that the defendant is automatically innocent. Even the worst investigation by the most incompetent investigators can still develop incriminating circumstantial evidence that leads to a person's guilt.

Police Corruption

Actual police corruption, although it does occur, is relatively rare. It takes too many people to complete a successful cover-up. It requires the cooperation of other officers at the scene, CSI personnel, lab personnel, evidence control, and higher-level management, as well as the filing of false reports. When it is discovered, many people are involved, and a complex web of individuals is often found to be part of a conspiracy. And hopefully rooted out of the organization.

The police corruption necessary, for example, to plant someone's blood or DNA, would require the assistance of the evidence vault, perhaps the civilian laboratory forensic scientists, police officers, CSIs, and other detectives at the crime scene, and the capability to transport that evidence to the scene. Another aspect to consider is timing. If a detective is, perhaps, planting a glove at a crime scene, they would have to be sure that the victim did not have a rock-solid alibi, or it would immediately come back to haunt the officer.

It is much more common for a single police officer or detective to make a mistake or misjudgment in their procedure and then try to cover it up. They may be reluctant to admit they made a mistake, accepted a mistaken witness ID, or misinterpreted some evidence.

DNA

In some trials, the defense may challenge DNA evidence, raising concerns about contamination, improper laboratory handling, police collection errors, and the possibility of false positives. There is a tendency among the defense to claim that, if the DNA does not match, the suspect must be innocent, even if other explanations exist for their DNA not being present. Criminal defense attorneys may argue that DNA may only exclude but cannot conclusively include or prove a suspect's guilt. Or, if the DNA matches the defendant, it may be unreliable or contaminated, or the lab testing was done by the state and cannot be trusted. Obviously, none of this is true; DNA, even when mixed with other profiles, can directly point to a single person.

Misapplied Forensic Science

Here is a pronouncement from the Innocence Project website about the misapplication of forensic science: "Misapplied forensic science contributed to more than half of our wrongful conviction cases and nearly a quarter of all wrongful conviction cases since 1989."

However, extensive research has been unable to verify this figure. Several of the statistics appear to have been manipulated to inflate the number of forensic science cases, including use of borderline proficiencies such as dog scent analysis.

Text from the Innocence Project website, under Misapplication of Forensic Science, lists several methods where they believe that, "in these cases, forensic science practitioners provided misleading testimony that exaggerated the connection between the crime scene evidence and the person of interest, mischaracterized exculpatory results as inconclusive, or downplayed the limitations of the forensic science method they had used." The methods listed are bite mark analysis, hair comparisons, tool mark evidence, arson investigation, fingerprint analyses, dog scent evidence, comparative bullet lead analyses, shaken baby syndrome diagnoses, and bloodstain pattern analyses.

This appears to be a conflation of proven legitimate forensic methods with others that are entirely subjective. Bite mark analysis, dog scent, and shaken baby syndrome can be highly subjective and up to interpretation. These should not be placed in the same category as hair comparisons (as shown below), tool mark evidence, and bloodstain pattern analysis, because the defense can easily elicit their limitations. Of note, and arson investigation have both reached a current state of limited scientific basis. Due to manufacturing inconsistencies, comparative bullet lead analysis, which examines the chemical composition of the bullets, must acknowledge potential limitations.

It is somewhat bizarre that the text includes fingerprint analysis, as research shows no legitimate fingerprint case in which the testimony was misleading, except for one instance in which the expert overstepped by discussing their observations on the fingerprint's freshness at the crime scene. However, there is a recurring theme whereby defense attorneys attempt to dilute fingerprint testimony, probably because fingerprints are so incriminating and difficult to dispute. In fact, among the millions, or perhaps billions, of fingerprint cases processed daily throughout history, the number of legitimate fingerprint misidentification cases is under 10.

There is a grand irony in the way innocence organizations give weight to forensic evidence presented in exoneration cases. The way they use forensic evidence itself seems misleading. The categories created for false and misleading forensic evidence are so broad that they encompass many general expert groupings. Additionally, discounting forensic evidence is rarely the sole contributing factor in an exoneration. In some cases, an appellate court may conclude that a new trial is warranted for other reasons, such as mistaken witness identification or inadequate legal representation, even if forensic evidence was presented at trial.

The Innocence Project published a 2022 report titled "The Contribution of Forensic and Expert Evidence to DNA Exoneration Cases." The report presents two perspectives on compiling the categories and defining the factors. The report lists all the various contributing factors to exoneration and acknowledges that multiple factors may work together to lead to exoneration. The factors in the report are: "1. Eyewitness misidentification 2. False accusation 3. False confession 4. Forensic evidence 5. Inadequate legal defense 6. Informant evidence 7. Police misconduct 8. Prosecutorial."

The number used throughout the report is 375 exonerations for the Innocence Project by 2020. That is the number to be divided among the various exoneration categories.

The report includes anecdotes from real cases, which are then applied loosely to these terms. The way the statistics are kept, these cases also include or have a significant reason for exoneration other than forensic evidence. The person may be exonerated based on DNA evidence, as the case initially relied on eyewitness testimony, and they also found misleading forensic testimony.

In the defense attorney world, misleading forensic testimony occurs when the expert makes a positive, conclusive statement about their examination. This may be inappropriate or from some fringe "forensic" categories. Still, some techniques that have been studied and proven for literally over a hundred years can be presented conclusively. Defense attorneys dislike these presentations because they directly implicate their clients.

The report suggests that even techniques outside the "common definitions of forensic science" should still be counted as misleading forensic testimony. These methods may include canine evidence and shoe rubber analysis, among others.

There are many times when someone with expertise in a subject may be called on to explain evidence and give an opinion about their field — a witness to explain how cell towers track phones or how a car GPS works. The report suggests that there could be another grouping of "expert" evidence to include those other categories.

There is also an analysis statement that says, "Should the NRE [National Registry of Exonerations] include cases in which expert witnesses made statements that were literally true, but potentially highly misleading? The most common examples involve experts who testified to microscopic hair comparisons and reported that evidentiary hair was 'consistent with' reference hair from a person of interest."

This testimony is literally true, but the defense world thinks that it is misleading. This creates a quandary for forensic scientists. How should they answer without telling the truth? Of course, the defense would want all forensic testimony, such as fingerprints, diluted and challenged so they have a path to dispute them, but the truth is the truth.

In fact, this type of forensic testimony was arrived at by meticulously examining all possible conclusions to avoid being misleading. The question is always: What is an appropriate conclusion based on the evidence, without stretching the truth? Often, if the defense attorney is competent, they will elicit testimony that explains the limitations of forensic testimony. In the case of hair examination testimony, the expert might readily concede that they cannot conclusively tell if the hair comes from the defendant.

For example, in the Kevin Shiel case listed in the National Directory of Exonerations, the fingerprint examiner was excoriated for stating that the fingerprint found on a showerhead appeared recent because it had not yet deteriorated. (This case is not discussed further in this book.) However, in general practice, a fingerprint examiner can sometimes tell how recently a fingerprint was deposited on a surface. An experienced fingerprint examiner can often tell whether a processed fingerprint is recent by how the powder adheres to the impression. It might be appropriate to inform investigators of that fact verbally, but it would be inappropriate to testify to that in court because there are so many contributing factors that there isn't an abundance of supporting research for that conclusion, only anecdotal experience.

CHAPTER 13

THE LANGUAGE OF INNOCENCE - LANGUAGE AND WORDPLAY

Just as language is powerful in the courtroom, language is also compelling and influential for the Innocence Machine. Both the prosecution and the defense use language to influence the jury or appellate judges to lean toward their side. Language can also be used in a coercive, deceptive manner. Defense attorneys may use *semantic infiltration*, which is a deceptive smokescreen that changes the words (language) in describing the case to minimize certain aspects of evidence and maximize aspects that they believe show the defendant's innocence. Techniques like this may be just *belief speaking*, in that they sincerely believe the statements. Or they may be purposely *gaslighting* the reader or listener.

Language can take a case and, using the Innocence Machine formula of minimizing evidence and witnesses, dispute DNA and fingerprint evidence, as seen in the cases of Marcellus Williams and Melvin Mikes. Or they may use the language to whittle the cases down to a lone witness, as in the Anthony Porter case; shoehorn in an element of police corruption, like in the Karen Read case; claim police racism, like the O. J. Simpson and Julius Jones cases; add a dash of police incompetence; and for good measure a SODDI alternate suspect, and the Innocence Machine is off and running.

Here are some examples of *innocence language* that can be found in text on websites describing the circumstances of various cases (emphasis is the author's):

"Subramanyam (Subu) Vedam has been wrongly imprisoned at a maximum security prison in Huntingdon, Pennsylvania, for 42 years for a crime he did not commit."

"He was held *without* bail *illegally* while awaiting trial, and in February of 1983, he was *wrongfully convicted* of the crime even though prosecutors produced *no tangible evidence* linking him to the victim's death. He was sentenced to life without parole."

"The case was based entirely on circumstantial evidence. There was no witness, no motive, no weapon, no exact date of death, and no direct evidence."

The language and verbiage used is highly misleading and in some cases incorrect. Vedam was not held illegally, and there was substantial evidence linking him to the victim's death. Circumstantial evidence is still strong evidence.

Here is some of the evidence presented at Vedam's trial: A bullet from a .25 caliber handgun was found with Kinser's (the victim's) remains, and police found a .25 caliber shell casing in the immediate area. Police learned that Subramanyam had purchased a similar handgun about a week before Kinser's disappearance. They also learned from witnesses that Vedam had test-fired the gun he purchased, and they went to that location and recovered a .25 caliber casing. Subsequent testing of the casing by ballistic experts determined that the casing and the casings from the crime scene were fired from the same weapon.

New Evidence, Bullet Hole Too Small

New evidence is occasionally used to revisit a case and submit a motion for a new hearing on behalf of the convicted person. There have been two instances of "new evidence" in the case of Subramanyan (Subu) Vedam.

The case is about the murder of Thomas Kinser in 1980 in State College, Pennsylvania, where Subu Vedam was the last known person to see him alive.

When Subu was arrested for the murder, the yellow yard signs around the town of State College, Pennsylvania, read "WE'RE FOR INTEGRITY/ #FairTrialFor Subu." The "Free Subu" website's slick presentation reveals the reasons why it claims Subu was wrongfully convicted. It says, "Newly discovered information was withheld during his previous trials–evidence he believes could prove his innocence." It is interesting to note that the website is surprisingly devoid of detailed circumstances of the case.

One piece of new evidence presented is centered around the size of the bullet hole in the victim, and another is the supposed withholding of transcripts of other people interviewed during the investigation of the crime.

It was established that on December 14, 1980, Kinser borrowed a van to drive Subu, a friend of his, over to Lewistown, Pennsylvania, to obtain drugs.

The vehicle was discovered on December 15th in the parking lot of Kinser's apartment building, but there was no trace of Thomas Kinser.

When police questioned Kinser's girlfriend and family, Subu told them conflicting explanations of what happened. He said Kinser's girlfriend had left him at approximately five o'clock, after paying him in drugs for the trip. Subu then told Kinser's mother that Kinser was probably traveling to the South because of the cold weather and that he had $200. Kinser's father also questioned Subu about what had happened to his son and about the drugs and the two hundred dollars, but Subu refused to tell him anything.

Thomas Kinser was listed as missing until September 27, 1981, when a body partly covered with debris was discovered by in a wooded area in Harris Township. The body was eventually identified through dental records as Thomas Kinser. A subsequent autopsy revealed a single bullet hole through the top of the skull.

A bullet from a .25 caliber handgun was found with Kinser's remains, and police found a .25 caliber shell casing in the immediate area. Police learned that Subu had purchased a similar handgun about a week before Kinser's disappearance. They also learned from witnesses that Vedam had test-fired the gun he purchased, and they went to that location and recovered a .25 caliber casing. Subsequent testing of the casing by ballistic experts determined that the casing and the casings from the crime scene were fired from the same weapon.

Subu Vedam was arrested in 1982 and, in February 1983, was convicted after a jury trial of the murder of

Thomas Kinser. The lawyers for Vedam appealed the conviction, and the appellate court ruled that Subu should be retired based on new evidence. In February 1988, Vedam was retried, convicted again, and sentenced to life in prison. In the second trial, more evidence of the drug use of the victim and the defendant was produced.

Much later in time, spurred on by activists, Vedam's new lawyers, in an October 2023 filing, said that new evidence was obtained and in the filing said the bullet hole in the victim was too small for a .25 caliber bullet. They wrote that it was a "physical impossibility" and that the wound was "simply too small" to be caused by a .25-caliber.

This certainly isn't a scientifically supported assessment of bullet wounds, and medical examiners well know that these measurements can vary wildly. An FBI forensic anthropologist said that there is no significant statistical difference in the holes created by a .22 and a .25. According to her, asserting a bullet caliber based on the size of the hole is "not advisable" and is an "unacceptable practice" in forensic anthropology.

The appellate court denied Subu's request for a new trial.

In 2024, Vedam's lawyers filed a request for a new trial, citing both the size of the bullet hole and the new evidence that some interviews of people conducted during the investigation were not disclosed to the defense. The filing claims that these items exonerate Subu Vedam.

This tactic does not appear to automatically exonerate Vedam and should be met with strong resistance from the scientific community. The bullet hole size concept is precisely what the defense would call an overstatement of forensic science had the prosecution used it in their case. It is pseudoscience and does not point to innocence. The other possible witnesses also do not exonerate Subu. This is a case of a huge stretch of potential evidence by the defense to attempt to exonerate their client.

Mary Yoder

Here is another example of language being used to project an appearance of innocence (author's emphasis added), from one of the Free Katie websites: "The American justice system failed Katie Conley on November 6, 2017. She is *innocent and unjustly incarcerated* while the person(s) responsible for Dr. Mary Yoder's death have literally gotten away with murder."

The Free Katie website continues: "Kaitlyn is a kind and gentle soul who would never harm anyone. She is without a doubt innocent in the murder of Dr. Mary Yoder. With everything going smoothly in her personal and professional life, Dr. Mary Yoder and her loved ones' lives turned around on the morning of July 20, 2015."

Evidence presented during the trial included Kaitlyn's computer history showing she had searched for lethal poisons on the internet, and she had created a fake Gmail ID, "mradamyoder1990," which was intended to lead to Yoder's son Adam, using his name, to make it seem he was the guilty one. This phony email ID had been used to order the poison. Police found that the poison was indeed addressed to Adam Yoder and was bought using a prepaid debit card. However, during an interview, investigators got

Conley to admit that she had purchased it. Results then came back from the police laboratory, and the report showed that Kaitlyn Conley's DNA was on the bottle of Colchicine found in her ex-boyfriend's vehicle.

Harold Hansen

Here is a quote supporting Melvin Mikes: "For Mikes, the card is a bittersweet memento of a chain of events that began in 1985 when he was arrested for a Long Beach murder he swears he did not commit. Mikes was convicted and sentenced to 25 years to life *based solely* on the fact that his fingerprints were found at the crime scene and on the murder weapon — a *turnstile bar that had once been used at the entrance of a hardware store.*"

Interesting use of the word *solely* because a fingerprint is unique, and it means the suspect had touched something, in this case, the murder weapon, found at the crime scene, but somehow had contact with it prior to the murder.

The bottom line is that there is a need for thorough scrutiny of all the evidence in every case, no matter the language on the "Free __" websites or the perspective of true crime documentaries.

Fingerprints On Murder Weapon Are Not Enough

When police arrived at Harold's Fix-It Shop in Long Beach, CA, on March 18, 1980, they found Harold Hansen bludgeoned to death. The shop had been ransacked, and the 76-year-old's pockets had been turned inside out. Investigators found three chrome sections of what appeared to be a disassembled turnstile. One three-foot section appeared to be the murder weapon. Long Beach CSI fingerprinted the section, and at least some fingerprints were observed and recovered.

Police determined that Hansen had purchased the turnstile at a hardware store's going-out-of-business sale approximately four months before his death. The turnstile parts were stored in the shop's basement and were not accessible to the general public. The fingerprints from the turnstile were then stored at the Long Beach Police Department.

In 1985, the fingerprints were searched in the new California Department of Justice's computerized fingerprint database, and a match was found. Once Long Beach police were notified, they compared and verified that *six* of the fingerprints recovered from the crime scene and on the turnstile piece were identified to a man named Melvin Mikes. Mikes was in the system because of previous arrests for shoplifting, car theft, and drug offenses.

Mikes was arrested and charged with murder. Mikes claimed he had an alibi: He was walking a union picket line around the time of the murder. The picket line was not far from Hansen's shop, but a union official said he was present.

His trial was held that year, and he was convicted by a jury in Long Beach Superior Court and sentenced to 25 years to life in prison. His lawyers unsuccessfully appealed his conviction through the California courts, then eventually appealed to the U.S. Court of Appeals for the Ninth Circuit.

In 1991, the appellate court overturned his conviction and remanded the case to the state courts for further proceedings. The court noted that Mikes' fingerprints *could* have been left on the turnstile prior to Hansen's purchase of the equipment.

The fact that the U.S. Court of Appeals, Ninth Circuit, ruled that Mikes deserved a new trial based on the assumption that he could have previously touched the turnstile in the hardware store where it was purchased is astonishing. It would mean that the prosecution must always show that there was absolutely no previous access to a murder weapon by the defendant, no matter how farfetched it may seem. This should be left to the jury to decide whether the access seems reasonable or outside normal circumstances.

Just as the defendant is asking us to believe that somehow, some way the defendant was in that hardware store and happened to touch the murder weapon months before the incident, then conversely, it should be considered that the defendant could have possibly left the picket line to commit another burglary at the shop. The second scenario seems more likely, and the fact that there were no witnesses and his fingerprints were not on any other items is very common in crimes such as this and is not exculpatory.

The fact that his fingerprints are on the murder weapon is much more persuasive than the alternative and should not automatically lead to innocence. A fingerprint is definitive, conclusive, without a doubt (beyond a reasonable doubt) evidence that the person was there or the person touched that item.

Again, the fingerprints in the case were not some smudged, barely visible single impression. There were *six* fingerprints of the defendant on the murder weapon. The metal part was also located in an inaccessible part of the store and had previously been in another store, where it is doubtful that Mike had visited. This is a coincidental stretch beyond comprehension.

Innocence activists discounting fingerprints presents a definite problem with the approach to innocence. While there is a campaign within the defense community to dilute fingerprint testimony because it is such strong evidence and they often lose cases because of it, a fingerprint stands alongside DNA as one of the most definitive forms of evidence in the criminal justice system.

CHAPTER 14
SYMPATHY FOR A CAUSE: INNOCENCE CASES

One of the most egregious examples of *semantic infiltration* is one on a website discussing the Leonard Peltier case (emphasis added by the author).

"Leonard Peltier, now in his twenty-fourth year of confinement, was *wrongly convicted* of the murder of two FBI agents and has been *doing hard time* ever since. Peltier remains in prison as his appeals for clemency languish on the president's desk, despite calls for his freedom from the Dalai Lama, Desmond Tutu, the European Parliament, and other prominent international figures. Prison Writings, compiled by Peltier over the years, tells the extraordinary story of his life — his impoverished upbringing in the Dakotas, his gradual development as an American Indian leader during the political upheavals of the late 1960s and early 1970s, and the tense battles with the government that culminated with the 'Incident at Oglala.' This last event is one of the darkest moments of American history, when *FBI agents raided an Indian reservation on the slimmest of pretenses, setting off a firefight in which two agents were killed....* Peltier's trial was fraught with controversy and has been widely criticized for its numerous irregularities and injustices.

"*Correctly anticipating an unfair judicial process,* Peltier escaped to Canada following the shootout. *Using false information gained by intimidating a young Indian woman* into providing *untrue* testimony, the *FBI illegally* extradited Peltier from Canada and then withheld exonerating information at his trial. Since his conviction, a government lawyer has *admitted that the prosecution had no idea who killed the two FBI agents,* yet Peltier is still locked up at Leavenworth penitentiary in Kansas. Peltier is remarkably philosophical and even forgiving; his voice is a blanket of mercy and compassion. Looking beyond himself, he places his experience in the context of the long history of America's betrayals of and injustices to its Indian peoples."

Read all the contradicting evidence to the above paragraphs in the next section about the vast incriminating evidence, including the weapon Peltier held and used, and the stolen rifle a fellow shooter used in the murder of the FBI agents. Also of note, Peltier admitted on TV that he shot at the agents.

AMERICAN INDIAN CAUSE

In 1975, Leonard Peltier, a Native American, traveled with members of the American Indian Movement (AIM) to the Pine Ridge Indian Reservation in South Dakota from an AIM convention in Farmington, New Mexico. At that time, Peltier had an arrest warrant from Milwaukee, WI, for the attempted murder of a Milwaukee police officer.

On June 26, 1975, FBI Special Agents Ronald Williams and Jack Coler were searching Pine Ridge for a person suspected of assault and theft. Around 11 a.m., the agents, each in their government vehicles, pulled over an orange and white Chevrolet truck they thought might be the one they were looking for.

The vehicle stopped off US 18 at the Jumping Bull Ranch property, where members of AIM were camping. The occupants of the vehicle, Leonard Peltier, Norman Charles, and Joe Stuntz, exited and began shooting at the FBI agents.

Agent Williams radioed that they were under fire from the vehicle's occupants and would be killed if reinforcements did not arrive. Then Williams radioed that he and agent Coler had been shot. Another FBI Special Agent, Gary Adams, and some BIA (Bureau of Indian Affairs) officers responded and also came under fire from rifle and automatic weapons from the occupants of the Chevrolet.

The responding officers were prevented from reaching the agents, kept away by the gunfire from a British .308 rifle that had been reported stolen, fired by Norman Charles, and an AR-15 assault rifle fired by Leonard Peltier. Eyewitnesses later confirmed this fact.

FBI agent Adams and two BIA police officers were pinned down by fire from the two shooters and also from fire from other people on the ranch. Eventually, other law enforcement officers arrived, and they were able to get to the fallen agents at about 4:30 that afternoon. When they did, they found that the agent's weapons, their handguns, a .308 rifle, and a shotgun had all been taken, and Agent Williams' car was driven further into the Jumping Bull property and stripped of parts.

After further investigation, it was discovered that the two FBI agents had fired a total of five shots: two from Williams' handgun, one from Coler's handgun, one from Coler's rifle, and one from Coler's shotgun. Around 125 bullet holes were found in both the agents' vehicles, most from a .223 Remington AR-15 rifle.

A pathologist's report showed that SA Williams received a defensive wound to his right hand from a bullet that passed through his hand into his head. Williams was shot in the body and foot before the lethal contact shot to the head. SA Coler, injured from earlier bullet wounds, was shot twice in the head. These shots were determined to be at close range with the AR-15. Ostensibly, the AR-15 witnesses said Peltier carried.

Joe Stuntz, another occupant of the orange vehicle, was found wearing Agent Coler's FBI jacket after he was shot and killed by a BIA agent later that day.

There was testimony that Peltier, who was not from the Pine Ridge Indian Reservation, was part of a group that may have committed burglaries on the reservation where the British .308 rifle was reported stolen. Testimony also established that Peltier was the only person carrying an AR-15 rifle at the time of the shooting. One .223 shell casing was found in SA Coler's trunk, which was later matched to the AR-15 found later, as were the one hundred and fourteen .223 shell casings from the scene.

Court testimony described Peltier as carrying out one of the agent's handguns from the shooting scene, and one of the handguns was later found in a vehicle near the arrest of another person, said to be at the scene.

On September 6, two other people reported to be present near the shooting were injured in an explosion of ammunition from a station wagon, bought by Peltier, on the Kansas Turnpike close to Wichita. SA Coler's .308 and an AR-15 were found in Peltier's burned vehicle.

It was determined that on September 9, Leonard Peltier was traveling in an RV toward Canada, and after the FBI had broadcast a BOLO for the vehicle, an Oregon State Trooper stopped the RV. The trooper described Leonard Peltier as having exited the vehicle, fired at him, and fled. The trooper wasn't sure what weapon Peltier had used to shoot at him with, but Peltier got away. A search of the RV revealed SA Coler's handgun. The gun was fingerprinted, and a print was identified to Leonard Peltier. Other weapons and even explosives were also found inside the vehicle.

Peltier fled to Canada and was eventually located, extradited, and returned to the U.S. to stand trial. In April 1977, Peltier was convicted on two counts of first-degree murder and sentenced to two consecutive life terms. In 1979, he received an additional five-year sentence after a failed prison escape.

In a September 1991 *60 Minutes* TV program, Leonard Peltier was interviewed, and he admitted that he had shot at the agents during the 1975 incident, but he said he was not the one who killed the agents. Most of the program was about the obviously poor living conditions of indigenous people on the reservation.

This is interesting and significant because under felony

murder laws, even someone present at a murder while committing a crime, in this case, shooting at the FBI agents, can be convicted of the murder that occurred during that crime. Therefore, even if Peltier didn't personally shoot the FBI agents, though evidence shows the .223 weapon Peltier carried did kill them, he is still guilty under the federal felony murder statute.

During Peltier's imprisonment, people all over the world protested his innocence and called for his release. There was a Free Peltier T-shirt, a "freeleonardpeltiernow" website, an International Leonard Peltier Defense Committee, and Amnesty International called for his release. Most of the protests listed untrustworthy witnesses and government conspiracy as reasons for his "unjustified conviction."

On January 19, 2025, President Joe Biden commuted Leonard Peltier's sentence to indefinite house arrest before leaving office. On February 18, the date specified by the grant of clemency, Peltier was released.

Even if Peltier didn't shoot and kill the FBI Agents, he admitted he was guilty of firing a gun at law enforcement during that incident, and he was actually guilty of murder due to the federal felony murder law. He was also guilty of shooting at the state trooper and possession of a firearm, having put his fingerprint on one of the agent's weapons.

Is a cause sufficient to disregard the evidence and deem the convicted innocent? While the plight of indigenous American people is genuinely horrible, Leonard Peltier, based on his record, was not an innocent person in his life in general. And, based upon the evidence, the witnesses, and his own statements, he was also not innocent in the murder of two FBI agents in 1975.

MURDER FOR A CAUSE?

Luigi Mangione was accused of killing United Healthcare CEO Brian Thompson. The shooting was captured on video outside the New York Hilton Midtown hotel near MoMA and Rockefeller Center.

Mr. Thompson was shot from behind on December 4, 2024, while on his way to a UnitedHealth Group investor conference. Local video footage showed a gunman walking up behind Mr. Thompson, pointing a handgun fitted with a suppressor, and shooting him in the back. Mr. Thompson then can be seen scrambling away, but the gunman continues shooting him and then runs away with a large backpack. Later examination showed Thompson was shot once in the back and once in the leg.

Police at the scene recovered several bullet cartridges left on the sidewalk, which had the words "deny," "defend," and "depose," written on them, possibly references that have appeared in activist writings to the delay tactics health insurance companies can use to stall paying claims.

Due to the high profile of this case, the NYPD discovered various video segments following the shooter on his journey, fleeing through the city. They found video of him seen entering Central Park, ditching the backpack, then riding a bicycle down Columbus Avenue, ditching the bike, and eventually getting into a taxi on Amsterdam Avenue. Then, another video picked up the shooter at the bus station. It appeared that he had taken a Greyhound bus. The man in question was determined to be Luigi Mangione, 26 years old.

Police were also able to backtrack Mangione's time in New York, prior to the shooting, and found a smiling photo of him at a hostel where he stayed. This photo, which the NYPD circulated, was said to have led to his sighting at the McDonald's in Altoona on December 9th.

Among Mangione's possessions was a backpack containing a 9mm handgun and a separate silencer with parts that had been made on a 3D printer. The gun taken from Mangione had a loaded Glock magazine and was later determined to be a ballistic match to the ejected 9mm rounds found at the crime scene. They also located his computer and a notebook with writings from Mangione.

Further forensic examination of some items discarded by Mangione as he fled across Manhattan identified his fingerprints on a water bottle and a health bar wrapper found along his route toward the bus station.

In addition to the New York cases, Mangione also faced criminal charges of carrying a firearm without a license, forged documents, and other charges in Pennsylvania, where he was arrested.

Since Mangione's arrest, thousands of people have been calling for reform of the country's healthcare system. They have called Mangione a hero. People have carried Free Luigi banners and signs. The Luigi Mangione defense fund has raised almost $700,000. There were Mangione supporters wearing face masks and green Luigi hats from the Super Mario video game. They have established several supporting websites and a Free Mangione Official Facebook page.

In the crowd of a rally organized outside the Lower Manhattan courthouse where a hearing was to be held, some people handed out fliers trumpeting support "for people harmed & killed by insurance industry greed."

Reviewing the signs and placards at the protests for Luigi Mangione, many of them are actually protesting the poor condition of health care in the U.S., not directly supporting Mangione. There is an emphasis on changing health care, and Luigi Mangione has become the poster boy for the movement, even while ignoring the viciousness of the crime.

Is a moral or social cause sufficient to overlook violence in order to advance the cause? Is it sufficient to ignore a murder? Or is a cause adequate to minimize a murder for the sake of the cause?

CHAPTER 15

MISFIRE OF INNOCENCE ADVOCATES

Cases have been found where the Innocence Project or local innocence projects successfully released someone, only for them to go on to commit further crimes. Such as the cases of Yathomas Riley (discussed previously) and the Shaurn Thomas (discussed next), where the released person went on to kill the main person responsible for his release.

What does it mean that, according to Milwaukeemagazine.com, 174 Innocence Project exonerees have later been charged with violent crime? Though this number is suspect and may be a misinterpretation of other statistics, what is the correct number? This book contains several cases where this did indeed happen.

The 174 number actually seems to be a confusion of a statement on the Innocence Project website that says "165: Actual assailants identified. Those actual perpetrators went on to be convicted of 154 additional violent crimes, including 83 sexual assaults, 36 murders, and 35 other violent crimes, while the innocent sat behind bars for their earlier offenses."

There are many complaints by the general public about criminals with long rap sheets that are released and then go on to commit further crimes, even murders, and multiple murders, as in the case involving William Reece (discussed previously).

Is the reason judges give sentences like life plus 50 years that they believe that

appellate attorneys will try to get these criminals paroled or released?

The question has to be asked: Why are appellate attorneys searching for technical violations and procedural errors when 1) the defendant may really be guilty, and 2) they may be released to commit further crimes against the public?

Shocking Murders after Release

Shaurn Thomas was convicted of a 1990 murder and was sent to prison. In 2017, a judge vacated his conviction after the Pennsylvania Innocence Project helped bring forward issues with the police investigation. The issues surrounded an incomplete police investigation and police interrogation tactics. According to the *Philadelphia Inquirer*, prosecutors said they weren't 100% convinced that Thomas was completely innocent of the killing, but the Philadelphia District Attorney's Office declined to retry his case.

When Thomas was released, he became a shining example for the wrongly convicted and was listed on the

Pennsylvania Innocence Project website. He became a millionaire after receiving a $4.1 million payout.

Thomas became acquainted with other exonerees and asked Ketra Veasy, whose brother was wrongfully convicted, to connect him with someone to sell cocaine, and she arranged for him to meet up with Akeem Edwards. According to the *Philadelphia Inquirer,* Thomas gave Edwards the drugs and asked him to bring in $1200 in profits, but Edwards never paid him.

In January 2023, Veasey and Thomas were driving through a neighborhood and spotted Edwards. According to Veasey, Thomas got out of the car and shot Edwards.

When questioned, Veasy said Thomas told her Edwards was his "third homicide" and "he can't go back to jail." He then warned her to keep quiet about the killing "or else."

On the statement of a federal informant, Philadelphia homicide detectives learned that Thomas had talked to him about the murder and was planning a hit on Veasy. Police then searched Thomas' home, where they found several weapons.

Thomas was arrested and charged with the murder of Akeem Edwards because he failed to pay him the $1200. He pleaded guilty and, in court, admitted to the murder.

The *Inquirer* reported that the judge at the plea hearing appeared nearly stunned by the facts of the case — that a multimillionaire who spent almost half his life in prison would risk being sent back over a comparably measly amount of cash.

Shaun Thomas was sentenced to 33-66 years in prison for the murder of Akeem Edwards.

Innocence activists had obtained the release of this man only for him to commit murder again after his release. This case raises questions about how many of these exist. How many murderers have been released by the Innocence Machine only to kill someone else?

Celebrity Rapper with a Gun?

A consistent thread exacerbated by the Innocence Machine is the release of convicted criminals who go on to commit crimes. One aspect of this is the practice of placing criminals on probation instead of prison, and while out on probation, they commit further crimes. Some might argue that they should have been sent to prison rather than given probation, so that this prevents further recidivist crimes.

The Meek Mill situation is a case in point.

Before his release from prison, there were Free Meek rallies, #freemeekMill posts, and celebrity backers like Kevin Hart, Jay-Z, and an owner of the Philadelphia 76ers. Mill is a rapper who has had success in the music industry, even impressing Questlove with his talent. He produced five albums and headlined three tours. Mill's supporters called for his release because he shouldn't have been sent to prison for a probation violation.

The Innocence Machine language in the Mill case refers to the fact that Mill was sentenced to prison for a "probation violation" when, in reality, he was sentenced to prison for several crimes. By using this language, the crimes are ignored, and people only react emotionally to the issue of probation. That language of "being sent to prison for a probation violation" is repeated throughout the messaging of the Meek Mill campaign. Those who were sent to prison after they violated probation by committing a further crime are probably wondering why they can't be released, too.

When people are convicted, they can be sentenced to prison or placed on probation. On probation, a criminal is free from a prison sentence but must obey specific rules; if they fail to do so, they will be sent back to prison to serve their original sentence for the crimes.

Make no mistake, Mill committed multiple crimes. Let's delve into this case without the biased language.

In 2006, Mill was convicted of illegally possessing a firearm. Police said he walked into a store with a gun, and according to the arresting officers, he pointed that gun at them and tried to shoot them before they could subdue him. This first conviction resulted only in probation.

In 2009, Mill was convicted of second-degree possession of a loaded firearm by a convicted felon (note "convicted") and possession of drug paraphernalia. On these convictions, the judge sentenced Mill to 11 to 23 months in prison, followed by 8 years of probation. It is important to note that, although one can't be sure in this case, typically the original charges in many cases are possession of a firearm by a convicted felon and possession of illegal drugs that are negotiated down to second-degree charges and possession of drug paraphernalia.

Mill was given an early release in 2009 after serving only 7 months, but it was agreed that he would be on parole for 5 years. Convicted felons typically sign a release agreement and are given instructions about the rules of their probation. They are paroled on certain conditions that they must meet or else go back to prison, and every convicted person should know that.

After Mill's release on probation, he was found to have violated his probation in 2012, 2013, 2014, 2015, and 2017. On November 6, 2017, he was sentenced to 2 to 4 years in state prison for violating his parole. He served only 5 months, and in 2018, he was released on appeal. In 2019, he was granted a new trial by the Pennsylvania Supreme Court. That year, Meek Mill pleaded guilty to a lesser charge of misdemeanor possession of a firearm; as a result, he was no longer a convicted felon.

After his release, Mill gave frequent interviews in which he talked about the violence of his upbringing, implying that at least some of his crimes were influenced by that violence. He also pointed to photographs of beatings by the police. Is exposure to violence, a violent upbringing, an excuse for committing a crime?

Additionally, in a couple of the incidents, the police officers stated that Mill pointed a gun at them. One can imagine how angry the police officers were after being threatened with a gun, especially knowing that police officers are shot almost every day in the United States. Is this an excuse for the police to beat a suspect?

Misdirection & Murder by Colchicine

A documentary about the Kaitlyn Conley case on HULU is titled *Little Miss Innocent: Passion. Poison. Prison.* One may obtain a yard sign that reads "Free Katie Conley" from the Free Katie Conley website or the Facebook page, which states, "Wrongful convictions happen."

The evidence is this: In July 2015, Dr. Mary Yoder, a 60-year-old chiropractor, began feeling sick while working in her chiropractic clinic in upstate New York. The next morning, she was admitted to the hospital. Doctors could not determine what was wrong with her. She was set for discharge the next morning. However, on July 22, 2015, Mary suddenly went into cardiac arrest and was declared dead at the Faxton-St. Luke's Healthcare Center in Utica.

Police investigators did not immediately know what kind of case they had at first, but they had a suspicion that Mary Yoder had been poisoned. After her body was examined and blood testing was conducted, tests came back that showed she had been given a lethal amount of an unusual poison, colchicine. The medical opinion was that colchicine poisoning happens within a short time frame, and, most likely, Mary was given the substance during her last day at work. Police then launched a homicide investigation into the death.

They naturally suspected Mary's husband, William Yoder, and looked into his whereabouts at the time of the murder. After determining his relevant locations on the day that Mary had become sick and looking for any possible motivation, he was cleared, at least temporarily, of the crime.

That November, the police received an anonymous letter that blamed Mary Yoder's son, Adam, for the murder of his own mother. Within the letter was even the location of a colchicine container. The letter said it could be found under Adam's passenger seat in his Jeep. This led police to question Adam in December 2015.

Adam told the investigators that he did not know anything about any poison, and allowed the police to search his vehicle. Upon searching the messy vehicle, they found a bottle of colchicine, tucked inside a paper wrapper, under the passenger seat, exactly as described in the letter.

Police investigated Adam's whereabouts on the day that his mother had become poisoned and learned that he had visited one of his sisters in Long Island. These family interviews raised investigators' suspicions about the anonymous letter.

Since the poisoning most likely happened during Mary's workday, police also interviewed the receptionist at the chiropractic practice. Kaitlyn Conley had been employed at the office for about four years. Conley told them she and Mary had lunch together that day. Police also learned that Kaitlyn was Adam's former girlfriend. After a lengthy interview, Conley eventually admitted she had sent the letter to the authorities because she believed Adam was responsible. She said she had seen the vial in Adam's car.

Police investigators dug into Conley's computer history and found out that she had searched for lethal poisons on the internet. They also discovered that she had created a fake Gmail account, "mradamyoder1990," which was intended to lead to Adam. Then they found that this fake email ID had been used to order the poison. Police found that the poison was addressed to Adam Yoder. Police found that the poison was bought using a prepaid debit card, and, during an interview, investigators got her to admit that she had purchased it.

Results then came back from the police laboratory, and the report showed that Kaitlyn Conley's DNA was on the bottle of colchicine found in her ex-boyfriend's vehicle. Conley was arrested in June 2016 and charged with the second-degree murder of Dr. Mary Yoder.

In April 2017, Kaitlyn Conley was tried for the murder of Mary Yoder. After the courtroom presentation of evidence and the defense's response, the jury was found to be deadlocked, resulting in a mistrial. The prosecution arranged a second trial. On November 6, 2017, the jury returned with a guilty verdict, and Conley was convicted of first-degree manslaughter. The following January, Kaitlyn Conley was sentenced to 23 years in prison with the possibility of parole.

In addition to the websites, a *Dateline* episode was dedicated to the Kaitlyn Conley case in 2023, and the HULU film *Little Miss Innocent* was released in 2024.

After a number of appeals were denied over the years, Conley's lawyers, arguing that she had ineffective counsel during both her trials, obtained a ruling from an appeals court that Conley's first trial lawyer provided ineffective counsel after failing to challenge the admission of evidence pulled from Conley's cell phone. It appears that the search warrant was not specific enough to retrieve the desired information from the phone. The Oneida County Sheriff's Office used the evidence found on her phone to elicit a confession from Conley that she had purchased a prepaid debit card to buy the poison. Based upon this ruling,

Kaitlyn Conley's conviction was overturned, and she was granted release from prison.

The Oneida County District Attorney is considering a new trial for Kaitlyn Conley, as all the other evidence remains duly incriminating. Additionally, much of the evidence found on Conley's phone was also discovered on Adam Yoder's computer in a backup file labeled "Katie's iPhone," which reinforced what they found on Conley's phone.

It's interesting to note that sometimes the courts think that removing a single piece of evidence from the overall case is enough to change the outcome, even if all the other evidence is strongly incriminating. It is as if some appellate courts do not consider the other cumulative evidence against the defendant, just the matter presented in the appeal. In this case, there is still considerable evidence that leads directly to the guilt of Kaitlyn Conley in the murder of Dr. Mary Yoder.

Traveling in the Mountains

Another of the many innocence activist organizations is Centurion. Centurion is a non-profit organization with a website that states, "Seeking freedom for the innocent in prison." The website text proclaims that Centurion exists "to vindicate the wrongfully convicted." Centurion helped to release Darryl Burton on a murder case that was substantially witness-based. After his release, Darryl Burton wrote the book *Innocent: A Second Look*. Darryl Burton was an advocate for Dana Chandler and was interviewed for the NBC *Dateline* episode, "Deadly Obsession," about the Chandler case.

Dana Chandler was placed on trial for the July 7, 2002, killing of her ex-husband, Mike Sisco, and his fiancée, Karen Harkness. Sisco and Harkness were killed by multiple gunshots while in bed in their home in Topeka, Kansas. Upon investigation of the crime scene, police noted that nothing appeared to have been taken from the home, and there were no signs of forced entry.

Dana Chandler and Mike Sisco had undergone a four-year, highly acrimonious divorce process, with a court awarding Sisco full custody of the children and ordering Chandler to pay child support.

Upon questioning by police, Chandler claimed she was traveling in the mountains of Colorado at the time of the shooting, but her recollection of her specific travel routes seemed inconsistent to the police.

Chandler said she was at or near Rocky Mountain National Park at the time of the murders. When Topeka police reviewed video footage of the entrances and exits, Chandler's vehicle was not visible on the footage. When asked about any hotel receipts, Dana said she had slept in her car. In her interviews, Chandler was confronted about a purchase of two 5-gallon gasoline cans she had bought shortly before the slayings. A witness at a gas station along the route from Colorado to Kansas said they served Chandler during that time frame.

Cell phone records showed that Chandler had turned off her cell phone minutes after buying gasoline, and it remained off for the next 27 hours. This time frame aligns with the murders. Phone records indicated that in the months leading up to their deaths, Chandler called Mike Sisco and Karen Harkness about 700 times.

Both of Dana Chandler and Mike Cisco's minor children testified for the prosecution during the trial. They talked about the possible harassment. Also, their adult daughter, Hailey Sisco, recalled that her mom had told her she had thought about killing Michael Sisco. Hailey testified she believed her mother killed her father. She also testified that she met her mother at a restaurant and her mother told her that she had bought the gas cans on July 6, 2002.

The Dana Chandler case underwent several starts and pauses. Chandler was initially arrested in 2011 and convicted in 2012, receiving a life sentence. However, the Kansas Supreme Court later overturned the verdict after finding that the prosecutor had committed misconduct. A second trial took place in 2022, but the jury failed to reach a verdict, and a mistrial was declared.

During the trials, relatives and friends interviewed related that they felt Chandler was harassing Sisco and that Chandler had entered his home prior to the murders in spring 2002, during a time she knew her children would be out of the house. There was also a friend who said Chandler had told them that on June 8 and 9, 2002, about a month before the murders, she had spontaneously driven from Denver to Topeka.

In a third trial, all of the similar evidence was presented, and on March 7, 2025, a jury declared Dana Chandler guilty of the 2002 double murder.

The Dana Chandler case seems to be one of solid circumstantial evidence. All of it leads directly to her.

CHAPTER 16
NATIONAL REGISTRY OF EXONERATIONS

Michigan State University is behind the National Registry of Exonerations (NRE), an excellently compiled database that states that approximately 20% of the 3,381 exonerations have been due to DNA evidence.

In the database, there are categories for exoneration based on perjury or false accusation; official misconduct by police, prosecutors, or other government entities; inadequate legal defense, false confession; false or misleading forensic evidence; mistaken witness identification; and other related offenses.

According to the Innocence Project, eyewitness error is the single greatest cause of wrongful convictions nationwide, playing a role in 72% of convictions overturned through DNA testing. This is not a wholly unexpected statistic since eyewitness observations are notoriously varied. Prosecutorial misconduct, such as withholding evidence, accounts for approximately 30% of wrongful convictions.

Some of the categories for crimes listed are sex

offender registration, nonviolent misdemeanor, felony obstruction of justice, weapon possession, assault, drug possession, and solicitation of stolen property. There are 34 sex offender registration "exonerations" listed and 481 drug possession, 82 assault, and 29 nonviolent felony exonerations, for a total count of about 3659 (perhaps some fall into two categories).

According to the National Registry of Exonerations, which allows a filtered search of exoneration cases, a whopping 187 out of 230 cases are sex crimes. Over 81% of cases listed on that page are rape convictions, along with crimes like "aggravated sexual assault." There seems to be an extensive overrepresentation of sex crimes overturned in the database, including exoneration of people for registration as a sex offender.

There is a common statement in the innocence world that only about 3% of people in prison are wrongly convicted. According to information compiled from the Innocence Project Research Resources page, the percentage of wrongful convictions in the U.S. ranges from 1% to 6%. They state that this is based on "some studies" regarding general state prison populations. In comparison, the Georgia Innocence Project states that "studies estimate that between 4-6% of people incarcerated in US prisons are actually innocent.... Determining the exact rate of wrongful convictions is challenging due to the difficulty in identifying all cases of innocent individuals incarcerated and the complexities of the legal system."

One has to assume that the formula for arriving at these percentages is based on the ratio of exonerations to convictions. There are two problems with this. If that ratio is used, the country's total number of wrongful convictions would be far less than 1%. Two, there are so many factors that would fall into any calculation that it would be impossible to arrive at a really accurate number.

It is interesting to note that, upon closer examination of the NRE database, approximately 25% of those initially exonerated later pleaded guilty.

One significant finding from the database is that not all cases resulted in an actual exoneration, as indicated in the exoneration database. There are many cases in which an innocence organization took up the case, and the convicted person was released to receive a new trial. Due to varying factors, the prosecution in those jurisdictions decided not to retry the case. There are also cases that are still pending.

CHAPTER 17

THE APPEAL OF A HIGH-PROFILE CASE

There is nothing like the appeal of a high-profile case. It affects everyone, from the investigators to the judges and everyone in between.

Police Corruption, An Allure Impossible to Resist

For some attorneys, allegations of police corruption can become a powerful courtroom narrative — one capable of shifting attention away from the evidence and toward the conduct of the investigation itself.

Outside the courthouse during the trial, a large group of people proclaimed Karen Read's innocence. Websites described this as the Free Karen Read Movement. Some of their signs said "Stop the Corruption" and "Free Karen Read." There is also a website controlled by "Turtle Boy" That says Read is "completely innocent and is charged by corrupt cops covering up the murder of a fellow officer."

Karen Read is a Massachusetts financial analyst and

adjunct college professor who was on trial for killing her police officer boyfriend by hitting him with her car.

The circumstances of the case are that Karen Read and her boyfriend, John O'Keefe, were out drinking at various bars on a snowy evening of January 28th, 2022, when she drove them to attend a birthday party at a friend's house. Just before they arrived, an argument ensued, and she parked the car away from the house. O'Keefe got out of the vehicle, and Read started to drive away, but she backed the car toward him and apparently hit him. She then drove home.

When police interviewed Read, she said that they had been dating for about two years and that night they were out drinking at two different bars. They went from C.F. McCarthy's bar in Canton to the Waterfall Bar & Grill across the street. She said she dropped O'Keefe off at the Canton home of another Boston police officer after midnight, then returned to O'Keefe's house.

Police investigators located Read's 2021 black Lexus at her parents' house. According to prosecutors, they observed a broken taillight and marks on the rear bumper.

Karen Read was arrested February 1, 2022, for manslaughter and leaving the scene of a motor vehicle accident causing death.

Read's trial began in April 2024, with the prosecution presenting substantial inculpatory evidence. A Canton firefighter testified that, at the scene, Read had said to him, "I hit him, I hit him. Oh my God, I hit him."

Forensic experts testified that O'Keefe's DNA was discovered on Read's vehicle on the broken taillight and microscopic pieces of plastic similar to the taillight in the victim's clothing. The defense contended that the taillight was broken in the police garage.

The defense attorney for Read, Alan Jackson (who had previously represented Kevin Spacey in a 2016 sexual assault case) suggested that O'Keefe had entered the house and was assaulted there.

However, police had statements from at least 10 people who claimed they did not see him enter the house. An expert also testified that O'Keefe's phone, which was found under his body, shows that his phone did not move toward the house.

The defense suggested there was a police conspiracy, and that the DNA evidence was planted in a police frame-up of Read. They also suggested that, in an effort to find anything that stuck, O'Keefe's DNA could have gotten on the vehicle in another way aside from the car hitting O'Keefe.

During the first trial, the prosecution presented abundant incriminating evidence. The defense made some wild accusations of deflection, suggesting that the injuries to the victim were due to a feral dog and that someone at a house party had beaten him and was actually responsible for his death. The defense also challenged, apparently successfully, the DNA evidence of O'Keefe on the broken taillight of Read's vehicle.

In an effort to promote the feral dog theory, the defense had a medical professional testify in support of the dog bite theory — an incredible concept in itself and one without any scientific background.

A friend of O'Keefe's, who had been at the bar with them that night, testified that Read could be intensely jealous of other women around O'Keefe. And a Massachusetts State Trooper read several text messages found on Read's phone that were sent to O'Keefe that supported Read's jealous nature.

A big part of the notions of Read's innocence is the underlying premise of a police cover-up and conspiracy that is often a battle cry for the innocence craze.

The first trial of Karen Read ended with a hung jury, and the judge declared a mistrial in July 2024.

There were numerous unmistakable parallels to the 1995 O. J. Simpson trial in Read's trial. At times, it seemed that the Read defense was following the "Dream Team" playbook from Simpson's 10-month trial. For example, they asked the jury to dismiss the DNA evidence, reminiscent of O. J., where the defense said that everything was planted in a frame-up by the LAPD. The first Read trial was also a case in which the jury ignored all substantive inculpatory and incriminating evidence, resulting in a hung jury. (Of course, in the O. J. case, he was declared not guilty.)

Another similarity was that the suggestion was made that police corruption accounted for the inculpatory evidence. Additionally, a parallel was shown in the misogynistic comments of an investigating officer to try to get the jury to believe that they somehow tainted the investigation, which was similar to the O. J. defense suggesting that LAPD detective Mark Furman somehow tainted the investigation because of his racist statements prior to the case.

An interesting part of the Read defense was the suggestion that O'Keefe was murdered inside the Fairview address house, whether it was murder at all, because that would discount any idea that the case was merely an inadvertent accident.

Karen Read's second trial began in April 2025. There was a landslide of incriminating evidence presented by the prosecution in Read's second trial. Some of the prosecutions' opening remarks, paraphrased and summarized:

On January 29th, 2022, paramedics responded to a cardiac arrest call at 34 Fairview Road. In snowy conditions, the paramedics found three women standing around a man on the ground. Paramedics recall that Read had made the statement, "I hit him, I hit him." Read's friend will also say that Read said, "I hit him, I hit him."

The prosecutor continued, "The case is about science and data. Data and science will show what happened that night."

The data from Read's vehicle shows that she drove to the Fairview address, parked for a time, then drove forward, stopped, and reversed, with the data showing backward acceleration at 75 percent. She stopped and then drove away. In other words, the defendant, who had been arguing with the victim via text messages, drove away, reversed, returned to the spot where the victim was standing, then drove away again.

Data from John O'Keefe's cell phone shows his movement that night. It showed that he never went into the house.

The video from McCarthy's bar shows that Read had seven or eight drinks then put a glass under her clothes as she left. Read and O'Keefe then went to another bar, the Waterfall bar, where they had another drink, making at least eight drinks before they got into her car and she drove to a party.

The data on her Lexus shows they left the bar, drove around, and got lost. O'Keefe's phone shows a call to a friend, and she gives him a location near the parents of a former girlfriend of O'Keefe's. People in another car following the Lexus arrived at the same location. The people in that car went into the house.

John's phone shows he got a text from a friend in that house asking if he was coming in to the party. The friend then looked out the window and saw the parked car on the street. O'Keefe's phone then shows movement: He got out of the car, and only 20 seconds later, he fell. He never moved after that. The Lexus data corresponds to the phone data.

Read admitted they argued. She told a paramedic that she was sad their last conversation had ended in an argument.

Read's phone use after the incident shows that she was very angry at O'Keefe. One voicemail says, "John, I f---king hate you." She made almost 40 calls to his phone that night.

Then comes the possible cover-up, not a police cover-up, but Read then leaves another message that says, "John, nobody knows where you are." She calls her friend and says, "I left him at the Waterfall." She also said she was wondering if a snowplow had hit him.

Both sides agreed that someone, possibly Read, on that morning googled "how long to die in cold." Prosecutors contended that the search happened after Officer O'Keefe's body was found.

Then, Read asks her friend to come to her house. Her friend said Read was so drunk she couldn't remember what happened. Prosecutors also presented that Read mentioned to her friends that she had a crack in her taillight and wondered if she could have hit O'Keefe. When her friend arrived, she saw broken taillight. They drove back to the house and could not find John in the snowstorm.

Prosecutors also presented witnesses who said Read told them, "John didn't come home. We had a fight" that morning. And that Read had said to another witness, "What if he's dead? What if a plow hit him?... I don't remember anything from last night, we drank so much I don't remember anything."

Another friend joined them, and the three of them went back to the house once again. This time, Read got out of the car, and in the dark, she said, "There he is." The other women did not see him. Read ran directly to the spot, and they all saw the victim on the ground. They then called 911.

An emergency responder said that, while hysterical and inconsolable, Read repeatedly said, "I hit him. I hit him."

They moved the body to possibly attempt CPR, and the third woman picked up O'Keefe's phone and put it in her pocket. This warmed up the phone battery, and his phone shows the movement.

Police searched the area, and they found plastic pieces from the taillight. A police officer is sent to Read's residence, and a dashcam video shows him pulling up to the house, showing her car and the broken taillight.

The police searched the area again after the snow had melted some, and they found John's shoe and parts of the broken taillight.

Court documents showed that in the weeks before and even the hours leading up to that night, Read and O'Keefe were arguing, and Read had allegedly left obscenity-laced and hate-filled voicemails and texts on O'Keefe's phone.

Prosecutors also presented evidence that they found a broken cocktail glass and pieces of a taillight at the scene. They presented evidence that the taillight piece had most likely come from Read's vehicle, which showed damage, indicating a collision. A prosecution witness testified that O'Keefe's DNA was found on the taillight piece. They also found tiny pieces of plastic in O'Keefe's clothing.

The prosecution also presented the same incriminating evidence from both Read's vehicle and O'Keefe's phone, showing the movement during that incident.

A forensic toxicologist estimated that Read's blood alcohol content most likely would have been around .13, more than the legal limit.

A medical examiner, who has done thousands of exams, testified that the victim's head injury was most likely the result of falling backwards and hitting his head. And that the death of the victim was also a result of hypothermia (being left out in the snowstorm).

The prosecutor then said there had recently been a campaign of public statements and a documentary that presented Read's own statements, confirming the data about what happened. She admitted driving drunk, that she was angry at John that night, and acknowledged that she hit him. The prosecutor then shows a video from a documentary about the case where Read is interviewed and says, "I didn't think I hit him. I could have clipped him. I could have tapped him in the knee and incapacitated him. He didn't look mortally wounded as far as I could see. But could I have done something that knocked him out, in the drunkenness and the cold, and he didn't come to again?"

The defense presented theories that there had been a police conspiracy and cover-up, and that someone else, possibly one of the policemen in the house, had committed the murder.

On June 18, 2025, Karen Read was found not guilty of murder and manslaughter charges but was convicted of driving under the influence of alcohol.

The Form in the Night & the Dog Didn't Bark

One of the most reviewed murder cases in U.S. history is the Sam Sheppard case. Over the years, many people have campaigned for Sam Sheppard's innocence. It appears that with every generation, a new analysis and book emerge about the case.

In 1961, Paul Holmes, a *Chicago Tribune* reporter, published *The Sheppard Murder Case*, arguing that Sheppard was wrongfully convicted. In 1972, Jack Harrison Pollock published a book, *Dr. Sam: An American Tragedy.* A 1995 book, *Mockery of Justice: The True Story of the Sheppard Murder Case*, by Cynthia L Cooper and Sam Reese Sheppard (Sam's son), proposed to present the real murderer of Sheppard's wife. In 1975, a movie starring

George Peppard, titled *Guilty or Innocent*, was shown on television, based on the Jack Harrison Pollock book. And in 2001, a book by James Neff, *The Wrong Man: The Final Verdict on the Dr. Sam Sheppard Murder Case*, presented the conclusion that Sheppard was undoubtedly innocent.

On July 4, 1954, police responded to the home of Dr. Sam Sheppard to discover that his wife, Marilyn Sheppard, had been murdered in the upstairs bedroom of their home in Bay Village, OH, on the shore of Lake Erie. Sam Sheppard was interviewed and told police that he fought with a "bushy-haired" intruder who got away.

Sheppard stated that he was sleeping downstairs on the daybed in the living room when he heard Marilyn yell his name. He said he ran upstairs, where he encountered a form in their bedroom, was hit on the back of his neck, and was knocked out.

When he awoke, he took Marilyn's pulse and determined her to be dead. He then checked his son's room, found he was sleeping unharmed, ran downstairs, saw the form again, this time leaving through the back door, and heading toward the Lake Erie shore. Sheppard further said that he chased the form down the wooden stairs toward the beach, again grappled with the form, and again lost consciousness.

Shappard said he awoke this time missing his T-shirt and watch. Then he went back up the stairs into his house and called the local mayor. He said he didn't know if the intruder was male or female, nor did he provide a further description. Police noted that Sheppard had no blood on his person.

When investigators examined the body of Marilyn

Sheppard, they found that she was laying on the twin bed on her back with her legs spread, her feet between the wooden bars of the foot of the bed. Her pajama bottom was pulled down, and her pajama top was pulled up, exposing her body. The police speculated that she had been sexually assaulted; however, if an attempt had been made, it would have been blocked by the wooden bars of the bed.

Marilyn showed cuts on her face and head, and there was blood spatter around the room. An autopsy would later show that she had over twenty deep cuts on her body, and she had been about four months pregnant.

Investigators searching the home found Dr. Sheppard's medical bag in a hallway, tipped over with contents spilled out on the floor. When they looked in Sheppard's office down the hall, they found the desk drawers open and a couple of trophies disturbed. Drawers were removed from the desk and placed on the floor. All three drawers of the desk were pulled out but left in their original position within the desk. The top of the desk, which contained various items and writing materials, remained undisturbed. A display mug on top of the desk, where spare change might be kept, did not appear to have been touched.

The living room appeared untouched; however, the writing desk in the dining room was disrupted. The top swing-down portion of the desk was open but not many writing items were disturbed. Two small piles of items were on the floor. Nothing else in the room appeared out of place. They also found no apparent forced entry into the home.

When police traced Dr. Sheppard's route into the backyard, the Sheppard's' dog, Koko, barked, and they wondered why it had not barked at the intruder. As they searched, they found a small green bag with some jewelry and Sheppard's watch. The watch had a spot of blood on it, and Sheppard suggested to the police that the murderer had taken the watch off his wrist when he lay unconscious on the beach. Sheppard still had his wallet on his person. They did not find the missing T-shirt.

The trial of Sam Sheppard began on October 18, 1954, in a Cleveland courtroom. After many weeks of testimony, the jury began its deliberations on Friday, December 17. After four days, they returned a verdict of not guilty of murder in the first degree, but guilty of murder in the second degree. The judge sentenced Sheppard to life, with his first eligibility for parole in ten years.

As described above, in the years after the original trial, many books and media presentations proclaimed Sheppard's innocence and highlighted the intense media coverage in Cleveland, OH, before the trial.

In 1964, Sam Sheppard's conviction was overturned due to concerns about due process during his trial. The court found that there was apparent prejudicial publicity in the community. However, the Sixth Circuit Court of Appeals reinstated Sheppard's conviction, pending his appeal to the United States Supreme Court.

In February 1966, the U.S. Supreme Court heard oral arguments in the Sheppard case, with attorney F. Lee Bailey arguing on Sheppard's behalf. This case propelled Bailey into the spotlight and brought him the fame to take cases like the O. J. Simpson case. The Supreme Court eventually reversed the conviction on the grounds that the publicity surrounding the trial prejudiced Sheppard's right to a trial by an impartial jury.

Later in 1966, Sheppard was tried again, with F. Lee Bailey as his lawyer. Bailey raised many doubts about the evidence and professed Sheppard's innocence. In this new trial in November 1966, the jury quickly acquitted Sam Sheppard of the murder.

After his release, Sam Sheppard returned to his surgical practice, but it became controversial when two separate patients died after surgery. Sheppard retired from medicine and, in 1969, appeared as a professional wrestler under the name "Killer Sheppard." On April 6, 1970, Sam Sheppard died, alone, at the age of forty-six, of liver disease.

It is acknowledged that there was intense negative media coverage prior to the first trial. However, the same might be said of the positive atmosphere prior to the second trial, given the press calling for Sheppard's release and the U.S. Supreme Court's ruling. There was a segment of society that focused on the prejudicial media in the 1950s.

Nevertheless, all of the inculpatory evidence presented in both trials leads directly to Sam Sheppard and leaves little room for the ghostly "form" attacker scenario. There appears to be an apparent staging of the scene, with the drawers, medical bag, jewelry, and the victim's pajamas all arranged to suggest that a dangerous burglar was present.

A murderer trying to cover their tracks is always in a different place than the victim. They try to create a crime scene that serves as a distraction from themselves. They may stage the scene to make it appear to be the work of another crime. Sometimes, though, since they are not burglars or criminals, they do not know exactly how to do it. They may overturn drawers, but do not make a mess. They may leave the top of their precious office desk undisturbed. They may put jewelry in a bag, like a burglar would, along with their watch. They may create a suspect but keep it vague and mysterious. They may find themselves with a bloody shirt and not know what to do with it, so they have to stash it somewhere, along with the murder weapon.

Who steals a victim's T-shirt and a watch? The dog, Koko, didn't bark. The disturbance in the house appeared staged. The victim's positioning appeared staged. All of this needs to be considered when suggesting that Sam Sheppard was innocent.

Obvious Staging, But by Whom

The JonBenét Ramsey case is well known, especially to true crime aficionados. A young girl was missing, kidnapped, and murdered in her family home on December 25, 1996, in Boulder, Colorado. There was a long, bizarre ransom note, and lots of things that pointed to an intruder who killed her and escaped through a basement window.

Many books and documentaries support John Ramsey's quest to declare his family's innocence. John Ramsey even gave a lecture at 2024's CrimeCon in Nashville, explaining the reasons why his family is innocent and calling for more DNA analysis. Intriguingly, John Ramsey is still using the media to claim the family's innocence when a lot of the public already believes in the family's innocence.

Interestingly, most of the books, articles, and documentaries claiming the Ramsey family's innocence were written by people who were temporarily embedded with John Ramsey and became enamored with his quest, to the point of ignoring certain unexplainable aspects of the case. These presentations typically involve mental gymnastics to create a scenario that accommodates the case's unusual aspects.

For example, how did the intruder enter and exit the house? He must have come into the house through the basement window without disturbing a spider web and then used the luggage below the window ledge. But this seems illogical because he had to have passed through the front door to go up from the basement to the desk in the rear of the house to write the ransom note, up another set of stairs to the victim's bedroom, and then back down the stairs right by the front door on the way down to the basement.

Any claim of innocence needs to explain why the outside suspect spent so much time in the home, in the night while the parents slept, writing a very long ransom note that mentions the exact small amount of John Ramsey's Christmas bonus, then had gone up the front stairs to kidnap a sleeping (and quiet) Jon Benet, but left the note at the back stairs, where, coincidentally, Patsy came down every morning. The demand note that took at least 15 minutes to write was written on the notepads in Patsy's desk in a back hallway with one of Patsy's pens from that desk.

Also usually included in these warped scenarios is that the outsider smashed Jon Benet on the head with some hard object, then fashioned a garrot, using a small paintbrush and cords from Patsy's craft section in the basement, strangled JonBenét, and then hid her in a small, unused back room in the basement down a dark hallway.

These outsider scenarios also usually have the suspect using the small, half-opened basement window, previously described, to both enter and exit, instead of just leaving by the front door that he must have passed at least once coming up from the basement to the first floor and going up to Jon Benet's bedroom.

An objective analysis of all these facts may seem to suggest deliberate staging as a misdirection tactic to create an outsider who can draw suspicion away from the family.

Some of these adaptive outsider scenarios also suggest that the kidnapper somehow saw John Ramsey's pay stub for his bonus, which is why he included the exact amount in the long ransom note. As for the length of time the suspect must have spent in the home, theorists say he had already been there and had made the ransom note. Perhaps that is when he discovered Patsy's craft supplies and the brother's knife and learned how to navigate the house's strange layout. Another scenario is that the suspect accidentally hit JonBenét over the head and strangled her, used the craft items — a little paint brush, and a cord — to create a garotte to make it look like it was a cartel and not just a regular kidnapper.

A couple of facts that are often overlooked are that the parents stated the children were in bed, and although the young Ramsey son frequently had a bowl of pineapple before bed, he was already asleep when they got home from a party that night and skipped his snack. However, it was found that Jon Benet had pineapples in her stomach.

Also, a blanket from a dryer in the basement, down yet another hallway, was wrapped around Jon Benet when her father brought her body up to the family room on the first floor, completely disturbing the crime scene. Additionally, there was a large flashlight that Patsy did not recognize still in the kitchen area, and the brother's Swiss Army knife was found next to the body in the basement.

All of these pieces of evidence scream obvious staging. But did an outsider do the staging to confuse the investigation, or did people within that house do it to lead the investigation to an outsider?

Two other aspects of the case that should be noted are that John and Patsy refused a polygraph administered by the police/FBI, and that a local grand jury recommended an indictment, but the DA's office declined to charge the parents.

One significant aspect of the case is the recovery of unknown DNA from the victim's clothing. This DNA remains outstanding, and innocence advocates rely on this to point to an outsider.

In contrast to the outsider scenarios, as long as those are being proposed, there is a possibility that the DNA is actually from a factory packer. Patsy did say that she opened a new package of clothing for her daughter to wear that evening.

As a matter of interest, the 370 word note, which reads like something an older person living during the time of the SLA and Patty Hearst would write, has some innocence advocates pointing to an outsider because there is reference to action movies, such as "Don't grow a brain, John." They declare that, even though it looked like Patsy's handwriting, and a handwriting expert could not exclude her, it must have been a man, therefore an outsider who wrote it. However, in the same vein as the mental gymnastics dismissing all the staging, one might as well consider that John could have participated in writing the note. After all, they *both* appeared to be fully dressed, possibly in their clothes from the night before, when the police had arrived.

If one sets aside the compulsion to fit an outsider into the case, given all the staging and evidence, it is easy to see why some people point right back to the family as having some culpability in the crimes committed that night.

There are other innocence cases where DNA is the focus of the investigation leading to an alternate suspect. However, unknown DNA evidence does not automatically prove innocence. Is this another case of too much reliance on DNA for an exoneration?

An Inadvertent Photo Defeats Self-Defense

From the book *Why I Know Jodi Arias Is Innocent: The Jodi Arias Trial* by Sophie Mathai, to the Jodi Arias Innocence Discussion Facebook pages with three thousand eight hundred members, there have been a lot of calls for Arias' innocence. The slick, striking, glossy website Jodi Arias Is Innocent.com is extremely compelling, with multiple links to information about the case, including links to statements about a biased judge, a "Justice Denied," a perjury implication page, a presumption of innocence page, and a page about government corruption. The website features a list of at least 12 blog posts and a link to donate to Team Jodi. There is even a link to Arias' art. Above a colorful graphic text of "We are Team Jodi, and we will be Victorious," there is a page of sweet, smiling, wholesome pictures of Arias. The assumption about Jodi Arias, going into her trial and subsequent appeals, was that she was a sweet, young, beautiful girl who could not have harmed anyone.

On June 4, 2008, 30-year-old Travis Alexander was murdered while taking a shower in his home in Mesa, Arizona. Photos from his digital camera verified that fact.

On June 9, one of Alexander's work colleagues was concerned that her travel companion, who was going on a work retreat to Cancun, Mexico, had not arrived. The co-worker gathered a couple of her friends, and they went to Alexander's house and woke up Travis' roommates. They went into Alexander's room and found him dead in his shower.

Investigators searching Alexander's home found a digital camera in the washing machine within a washed load of towels. The camera was destroyed, but the memory card was still intact. Police would later be able to retrieve the images that showed Alexander and a woman, Jodi Arias, in various seductive poses. Photographs showed Alexander alive in the shower. The date and time was June 4 at 5:29 p.m. There was also a final photograph that looked as if it was taken accidentally, with a person hurt and bleeding on the bathroom floor. The photo showed a person's clothed legs and the body on the bathroom floor behind them.

Jodi Arias herself contacted the police to obtain information about the case, and she told them about their relationship. She said she had moved to California on June 8, and she was not in Mesa on the day of Alexander's death.

Friends of Alexander directed the police to Arias and stated that Alexander had broken up with her because she was becoming a little strange. They said that they broke up in June 2007. They also said that Arias moved to the Phoenix area from California after they split up.

Police investigators found a palm print in blood on a wall in the hallway to the bathroom. Later analysis would find DNA from both Arias and Alexander in the area of the bloody palmprint. Fingerprint examiners would identify that palm impression as the palm of Jodi Arias.

Back on June 5, an attendee of a conference in West Jordan, near Salt Lake City, Utah, met a woman named Jodi Arias and noticed that the woman had cuts on her hands and had changed her hair color from blonde to dark brown. Arias said she had just arrived on a road trip from California.

Police learned that Arias had rented a car for the trip, and the odometer showed 2,800 miles when she turned it in on June 7. The rental car agent noticed a red stain on the car seats, and the floor mats were missing. The rental car dealer had the car cleaned.

When questioned, Arias said she had spoken to Alexander that Monday on the phone, but she had traveled from her grandparents' home in Yreka, down through California, and then up to Salt Lake City. Investigators calculated that the trip would be shorter than the mileage on the rental car and that the time frame would be shorter than that required to travel the route she claimed to have taken. Arias said she went down to Santa Cruz, then got lost off Interstate 15, which runs from Southern California through Las Vegas and up to Salt Lake. Police know that throughout most of that route, the I-15 is pretty much the only main highway, and it would be unusual for anyone to get lost along the way. She said she didn't go to Arizona. However, about 18 hours were unaccounted for on her trip from California to Salt Lake City.

A work colleague in Salt Lake said that Arias told him she cut her hands on a glass at a restaurant during her trip. However, it was determined that the restaurant she mentioned does not exist.

Police found out that a burglary had occurred at her grandparents' and a .25 caliber gun was stolen while Arias was living there. The gun that was missing was the same caliber as the one that shot Alexander. Arias had only been at her grandparents' for a short time before she left on her trip.

In a subsequent interview, Arias told a detective that she was indeed in Mesa at Alexander's home and they were interrupted by a man and a woman crashing into Alexander's bedroom. She said these intruders were in black with masks, and she struggled with the assailants. She went into detail in describing what the attackers said to them in the act of killing Alexander. She showed the investigator a cut she had on her hand and said that the woman attacker had cut her in the struggle. Arias said they knew where she lived, so she was afraid to tell anyone. She said she was really scared; she didn't want her family to be hurt.

In 2008, Arias was charged with the premeditated murder of her on-again, off-again boyfriend, Travis Alexander, in Mesa, Arizona. It was not until January 2013 that she was put on trial.

During the 2013 trial in Phoenix, the prosecution presented evidence showing that Arias had sent an email on May 28, 2008, demonstrating that she knew about Alexander and a female co-worker's trip to Cancun.

Witnesses testified that Alexander had a stalker during that time, someone who was always after him. These witnesses stated that they believed it was Arias.

A medical examiner (ME) testified that Alexander had sustained 27 stab wounds, a slit throat, and a gunshot wound to the forehead. Some of the wounds were on Alexander's back. The ME also testified that Alexander had what are generally interpreted as defense wounds on his hands. The ME also said that the bullet wound would have entered his forehead and gone into his brain, incapacitating him. Therefore, he was not shot first but stabbed and cut first, then shot.

During the trial, Arias now said that she had killed Alexander in self-defense after he attacked her when she dropped his camera. She said she shot him with his gun, but he didn't die, and she implied that he was still after her, so she stabbed him.

The prosecutor presented information about the gun that was stolen from Jodi's grandparents. That Arias had moved up from Arizona to Yreka just weeks before the murder. And that the missing gun was the same caliber as the murder weapon.

An ex-boyfriend of Arias testified that when she visited him prior to her road trip, she asked him for and took two gas cans with her. Police found a shoebox of receipts that Arias had kept from her travels, but none for any trips to Arizona. The prosecution suggested that the gas cans would allow Arias to drive through Arizona without having to stop for gas and leave any trail of receipts.

The prosecutor presented the DNA evidence and the fingerprint identification. They argued premeditation because they surmised that Arias took the gun from her grandparents' house, got the gas cans, and scheduled the trip in preparation for the murder.

The defense presented the self-defense scenario. They also attacked the victim, playing an audio tape of Alexander sexting and suggesting he was abusive and also a pedophile.

Arias took the stand and testified on her own behalf. She claimed that she couldn't remember stabbing Alexander or slicing his throat, but she did remember the knife clattering to the floor in the bathroom. She admitted that she was the one who shot and stabbed Alexander, but said that it was because he attacked her for dropping the camera.

In May 2013, the trial resulted in a hung jury and was declared a mistrial. The jury had reached an 8–4 decision in favor of the death penalty. Arias was retried in March 2015, resulting in another sentencing mistrial. This time they were deadlocked 11–1 in favor of death.

To clarify, in the Arias case, the jury unanimously

found her guilty of murder, so there was no deadlock on her guilt. However, two separate juries deadlocked on whether she should receive the death penalty. So the judge sentenced Arias to life in prison without the possibility of parole.

Here is an example of the innocence language on the Jodi Arias Innocence Project website: "The state's timeline depended on their interpretation of crime scene evidence and a series of timestamped photos recovered from Alexander's camera, which had been found in the washing machine. Arias took photos of Alexander in the shower "seconds" before stabbing him, the prosecutor claimed, and when the camera fell to the ground, it took a few more photos "accidentally," as Arias dragged Alexander's dead body. But these "accidental" photos are dark and distorted, there's nothing to conclusively identify Alexander or Arias, and her supporters question the validity of the manually-added timestamps."

The photos are not dark and distorted; both Alexander and Arias are shown in full-body images. They can be conclusively identified. In the last photo, which is a little blurry, Alexander is seen immobile on the bathroom floor, with someone's leg in the foreground. There is no evidence that the digital timestamps were altered.

The Jodi Arias case is a prime example of an emotional submission to the appearance and presence of the victim, while accepting a slanted view of the evidence. The initial and subsequent lies are significant in this case, along with the apparent concealment of her travels, and her admission that she killed him. There is no doubt about her guilt.

CHAPTER 18

NEW EVIDENCE OR JUST OLD QUESTIONS

Often, the new evidence isn't really new, it is just a revision of existing evidence, or it doesn't exist or has no bearing on the convicted person's guilt or innocence.

Extensive Evidence or Shaky New Evidence?

Since January 2024, the Los Angeles-based Innocence Project has been advocating for Scott Peterson's innocence in his bid for a new trial. The L.A.I.P. proclaims to have new evidence that Laci Peterson, Scott's eighth-month-pregnant wife, was possibly abducted and killed after witnessing a burglary near the Petersons' Modesto, CA, home.

There have been at least two film documentaries, one released in 2016 and another in 2017, advocating for Scott Peterson's innocence. In one, Scott Peterson's sister-in-law, Janey Peterson, an innocence activist for Scott, showed her "murder board" with her version of the evidence and her timeline for the crimes. She also suggests that a burglary that occurred in the neighborhood around the time Laci vanished is the reason she went missing.

In the recent Peacock documentary, *Face to Face with Scott Peterson*, Peterson also proclaimed the burglary theory. Scott speculated that his wife, while running that day, may have seen something suspicious, gone over to investigate, and been abducted.

There have been books published on both sides of the innocence issue in the Peterson case including *Presumed Guilty: What the Jury Never Knew About Laci Peterson's Murder and Why Scott Peterson Should Not Be on Death Row* by Matt Dalton. On the other side, Peterson's sister, Anne Bird, wrote *Blood Brother: 33 Reasons Why my Brother Scott Peterson is Guilty*.

There have also been podcasts that seem to declare Scott Peterson's innocence. Some of these advocates appear to be at odds with the true crime community, as it is widely believed that the Peterson case is closed and settled, mainly based on substantial circumstantial information and the fact that Laci Peterson's body washed up on shore just miles from where Scott Peterson was fishing the day of her abduction.

On December 24, 2002, Laci Peterson's stepfather, Ron Grantski, reported her missing after her husband Scott Peterson told him she was missing. When Modesto police responded to the Peterson residence regarding the missing-person call, Scott told them he last saw his wife on December 24, 2002, at about 9:30 a.m., when he left to go fishing. He said Laci had planned to walk the family dog to a nearby park.

Police learned that at about 10:30 a.m., a neighbor found the Petersons' dog alone outside their home and returned it to the Petersons' backyard.

Scott said that when he returned home, his wife's car was there, but the house was empty. He found their dog in the backyard. Police contacted a neighbor, who said Scott had knocked on their door, asking whether they had seen Laci. The neighbor said Scott told him he had been golfing that day and had tried to call Laci. Later, a relative of Laci's would also say that, at the Peterson home that night, Scott said he had gone golfing that day.

Modesto Police interviewed Scott, who told them about his fishing trip to the Berkeley Marina, near Berkeley, CA, about 90 miles away from Modesto. They found Laci's keys, wallet, sunglasses, and purse in a closet in the Peterson home. They organized a search of the local park and the surrounding area.

The nationwide media picked up on the missing person case, and of course, there were several possible sightings, as there always are in such cases.

On December 30, 2002, a woman named Amber Frey called the Modesto police and said she was Scott Peterson's girlfriend. She said she had met Scott on November 20, and he had said he was a widower, and they had planned to spend Christmas together.

Scott had been helping with the search and had been on TV expressing his feelings about his wife's disappearance. He gave an interview on January 21, 2003, with a local TV station, addressing the rumors about an affair and a recent life insurance policy, and denied them both.

On January 24, Modesto Police held a press conference. Amber Frey told the media that she'd had a relationship with Scott Peterson and that he had told her about his marital status. Frey said she contacted police after seeing the case in the media.

On January 28 and 29, *Good Morning America* presented an interview with Scott Peterson, in which he stated that he missed his wife and had nothing to do with her disappearance. He said that he had told the police about his affair and had also told his wife about the affair. He mentioned that both he and his wife had taken out $250,000 life insurance policies on each other years ago.

Two people, walking their dog on April 13, 2003, found the body of a baby on the shore of San Francisco Bay near Richmond's Point Isabel Shoreline Park. The next day, a runner observed a body that had washed up along the Point Isabel shoreline. The second body was about one mile away from where the baby's body was found. On April 18, the bodies were determined by the coroner to be those of Laci Peterson and her unborn child.

Police, in their search of Scott's warehouse where his boat was kept, photographed and recovered several items of interest. Inside the small boat, they found a pair of pliers with a hair wrapped around the ends. They also observed a homemade concrete anchor in the boat and five separate rings of concrete dust that matched the shape of the bucket Scott said he used to make the anchor. Scott told police that he had used a 90-pound bag of concrete to make only one anchor and used the rest to repair a spot in his driveway.

Scott Peterson was arrested on April 18, 2003, while driving near a golf course in La Jolla, CA. Peterson's murder trial began on June 1, 2004.

During the trial, Amber Frey testified about her affair with Scott, and that on one phone call she had with him, he told her he was in Paris when he was really in town.

An FBI trace evidence expert testified that she matched the hair from the pliers on the boat to hairs found in Laci's hairbrush using mitochondrial DNA. Defense lawyers argued that mitochondrial testing is unreliable for DNA comparison. (It's not.)

The prosecution had a witness who testified that the concrete used for the anchor in the warehouse was not the same as the concrete used to repair the driveway, as Peterson had claimed.

A hydrologist for the United States Geological Survey testified that the currents in San Francisco Bay would be consistent with moving from where Scott said he was fishing to where the bodies were eventually found.

Laci's neighbors and relatives also appeared as witnesses for the prosecution, providing information about statements that Scott had made around December 24, 2002.

The defense presented witnesses who claimed to have seen Laci Peterson on the day she was reported missing and in the days that followed her reported disappearance.

During the trial, it was suggested that it was possible that Laci had been kidnapped, held until she had the baby, and the bodies were then dumped in the bay to explain why the baby appeared so developed. The defense had a fertility expert testify regarding this scenario, but the prosecution poked holes in his testimony after it was found that he had based his assumption on a faulty date of pregnancy.

On November 12, 2004, Scott Peterson was convicted of murder for killing Laci and second-degree murder for the killing of their unborn baby.

It is interesting to note that, in traveling the some 90 miles to Berkeley, Peterson passed many fishing lakes, but the bay was the first deep water along that route.

Based upon the evidence presented at Scott Peterson's trial, especially the discovery of the bodies within miles of where Scott was fishing on the day Laci went missing, and the DNA evidence, it is baffling why any innocence project would consider this case. The mental contortion necessary to accept the alternative scenarios is breathtaking. The required mental gymnastics to come up with a situation where burglars killed Laci Peterson and, hearing about the case, knowing that the husband went fishing, went not to that exact area, but to a spot on the shoreline where the current would take a body, and then it would drop off exactly there is beyond conception.

Is this a prime case of people ignoring incriminating evidence in order to make the situation palatable to alternative solutions? There is certainly no new evidence in this case that is significant enough to warrant reevaluation of this conviction.

New Evidence on Disassembled Window

Sometimes murky ethics are on display when new evidence is proposed in these cases.

Alex Murdaugh was convicted of the murder of his wife and son on March 2, 2023.

The buyer of the property where the Murdaugh murders occurred has recently come forward to claim that he has found new evidence that proves Murdaugh is innocent. The buyer says that despite having torn the structure down, he kept the door and window with the bullet holes from the June 2021 shooting. He says that Murdaugh was too big to have fired the shots.

It was June 7, 2021, when Maggie Murdaugh and her son, Paul Murdaugh, were found dead near the dog kennels on the vast Murdaugh property in Colleton County, near Charleston, South Carolina.

Police responded to a 911 call that night, and when they arrived at the Murdaugh dog kennel property, called the Moselle property, they found a crime scene with the bodies of two people and blood spatter on the kennels. Alex told police that he drove over to the property and found his wife and son shot. He said he called 911 right away.

During the investigation, it was discovered that the victims were most likely killed with a shotgun and a .300 Blackout assault type rifle. Maggie Murdaugh was shot multiple times with a rifle-type weapon, and Paul Murdaugh was shot twice with a shotgun. Police located .300 Blackout cartridges and shotgun shells in the home, along with several weapons, but not a .300 Blackout rifle or a shotgun that had been recently fired.

Police investigators examined the crime scene and took extensive measurements of the bullet impacts and the blood evidence. They also noted the location of the bodies.

The police investigators impounded Alex's cell phone and attempted to find Maggie's phone. They did find Paul's phone and tried to retrieve information from it. The following day, police used Apple's "Find My iPhone" feature, and Maggie's phone was found along a road near the Moselle property.

After extracting the information from the phones, there was a discrepancy between the calls on Alex's phone and the call record on Maggie's phone. Some phone records were missing from Alex's phone. One of those records was a call to Maggie on that day. Also on Maggie's phone was a text to her friend, in which she mentioned being suspicious of her husband.

Electronics experts reviewed GPS data on the phones and located Alex's phone near where Maggie's phone was found. GPS data on Alex's vehicle also showed that Alex had driven that night near the spot on the road where Maggie's phone was found.

The evidence on Paul Murdaugh's phone was significant. A video on Paul's phone was taken that night, possibly minutes before the murders, at the kennels. The video shows one of their dogs, Bubba, with a chicken in its mouth. The video shows Paul's hand and includes Alex's audio calling out to Bubba.

This phone video was of momentous importance because Alex Murdaugh had vehemently claimed he had not been at the kennel that day prior to finding the bodies.

On January 25, 2023, Alex Murdaugh was tried for murder. After a lengthy trial, on March 2, 2023, the jury found Murdaugh guilty, and he was subsequently sentenced to two life sentences.

It does not seem as if the "new" evidence in this case is significant or exculpatory. Supposed new evidence can generate interest and media coverage, but sometimes lacks merit. The phone video definitely places Alex Murdaugh at the scene at the time of the murders.

CHAPTER 19
THE GENERAL INNOCENCE CRAZE

Evidence of the innocence craze can be found in the many books published about the topic, such as *Framed: Astonishingly True Stories of Wrongful Convictions* by John Grisham and Jim McCloskey and *The Sing Sing Files: One Journalist, Six Innocent Men and a 20-Year Fight for Justice* by Dan Slepian.

The innocence craze propels the Innocence Machine. It appears popular to follow innocence cases. Trying to find a wrongly convicted person borders on being a fad.

A researcher can pull up almost any case and find people advocating for that person's innocence. In many cases, almost without exception, family members or friends are adamant that the defendant is innocent, even when little evidence has been presented during the trial to support that claim.

Websites

There are many websites dedicated to the exoneration of people who have been convicted. There are some dedicated to freeing a specific convicted or accused person, websites discussing the case, and websites accusing police of corruption, mishandling of evidence, and a deliberate conspiracy to convict an innocent person. In almost every single one of the cases reviewed in this book, there is a vast discrepancy between the evidence presented at trial and the re-creation offered on the call-for-innocence websites. A simple comparison is astounding in terms of the evidence description and the language used to discuss the case.

The Exoneration Project Website

Almost all of the websites in the Innocence Machine are extremely biased, and many podcasts follow the same model, an obvious irony since many of them attack police bias in the cases.

An example from the Exoneration Project is: "The police investigation turned to Hood when Hood's fingerprint was found in a stray piece of trash at the crime scene. Instead of letting an innocent man go free, the detectives in Hood's case doggedly pursued a wrongful conviction."

In this case, from a 1993 murder, crime lab technicians matched Tyrone Hood's fingerprints in the car where the victim's body was found to a Miller High Life bottle and a Löwenbräu forty-ounce. Around the time of the murder, Hood was arrested twice for aggravated assault — one of the incidents involved unlawful use of a firearm — and for battery and theft. He had previously served a year on probation for the weapons charge.

CHAPTER 20
INNOCENCE MACHINE GONE WRONG

The innocence industry, while founded on legitimate concerns about wrongful convictions, can at times create chaos within the justice system by elevating advocacy, media pressure, and public emotion above careful scrutiny of the evidence.

No, DNA Did *Not* Exonerate Him

On August 11, 1998, Felicia Gayle was found murdered in her home in University City, Missouri. Gayle, 42, was a reporter for the *St. Louis Post-Dispatch*. She was found in her kitchen having been stabbed almost 43 times with a butcher's knife.

Felicia's body was discovered by her husband, who observed that the knife was still lodged in her neck. It was later determined her body had stab wounds all over and defensive wounds to her hands and arms. Police found that Gayle's purse, jacket, and a Macintosh computer were stolen from her home.

In 1999, a man named Henry Cole was incarcerated with Marcellus Williams, who had started serving a 20-year sentence for robbing a donut shop. After Cole was released from jail in June 1999, he went to the University City police and said that, while in jail, Williams had confessed to him that he had killed Felicia Gayle. Some of the details he gave were not publicly available. Cole said that they had numerous conversations about the murder.

In November 1999, University City Police contacted Williams' former girlfriend, Laura Asaro, who told them that Williams had confessed to her that he had killed Gayle. Asaro gave police considerable detail about how Williams broke into the house and killed Gayle. Asaro also said that she had found Gayle's purse in Williams' car.

Police contacted a person who was in possession of the stolen laptop computer from the Gayle residence and he told them he had bought it from Williams.

Based on these details, police searched Williams' car and discovered items that belonged to Felicia Gayle. A *Post-Dispatch* ruler and a calculator belonging to Gayle were found in his vehicle.

Marcellus Williams was charged with Felicia Gayle's murder and put on trial. In August 2001, Williams was sentenced to death.

In subsequent appeals in the Williams case, DNA testing on the murder weapon, a knife, was requested and conducted. The DNA on the knife did not come back to Williams. However, it did come back to one of the prosecutors, who later admitted they had handled the knife.

A statement released by the Missouri Attorney General's Office said, "In this case, a new round of DNA testing proved the office was right all along; the knife in question has been handled by many actors, including law enforcement, since being found. "In addition, one of the defense's own experts previously testified he could not rule out the possibility that Williams' DNA was also on the knife. He could only testify to the fact that enough actors had handled the knife throughout the legal process that others' DNA was present."

The statement also said that "Other evidence that helped convict Williams "remains intact, and the victim's personal items were found in Williams' car after the murder. A witness testified that Williams had sold the victim's laptop to him. Williams confessed to his girlfriend and an inmate in the St. Louis City Jail, and Williams' girlfriend saw him dispose of the bloody clothes worn during the murder."

On September 23, 2024, the Missouri Supreme Court unanimously denied the motion, stating that there was "no credible evidence of actual innocence or any showing of a constitutional error undermining confidence in the original judgment."

Judge Bruce F. Hilton wrote in his opinion, "There is no basis for a court to find that Williams is innocent, and no court has made such a finding. Williams is guilty of first-degree murder and has been sentenced to death."

Supporters and the Innocence Project spurred numerous public pleas and media attention, but on September 24, 2024, Marcellus Williams was executed by lethal injection in Bonne Terre, Missouri.

Searching the case online, it is difficult to find all the evidence introduced at trial and on appeal outside the Missouri Attorney General's statement. Most entries profess that an innocent person was convicted and executed. Considering all the evidence, it is difficult to disagree with the Attorney General's statement of "no credible evidence of actual innocence" exists.

For example, the victim's personal items were found in Williams' car after the murder. A witness testified that Williams had sold the victim's laptop to him. Williams confessed to his girlfriend and an inmate in the St. Louis City Jail that he had committed the murder. Williams' girlfriend saw him dispose of the bloody clothes worn during the murder. All of the evidence in question was available at trial, including the fact that the police and DA admit to touching the knife without gloves. Therefore, the DNA that is said to exonerate Williams does not necessarily do that.

An Unforeseen DNA Match

Initially, Anthony Apanovitch's daughter, Elana Wells, and his supporters believed in his innocence, but after the DNA results came back, that changed. Apanovitch's daughter had a change of heart after she had sought for years to overturn her father's conviction of the 1984 rape and murder of Mary Anne Flynn.

After his conviction, Anthony Apanovitch had many supporters, including a number of relatives, many anti-death penalty activists, and even a Republican lawmaker who was sure that he was an innocent man. This approach was displayed on the Justice for Tony Apanovitch website and in various innocence documentaries and YouTube videos.

Cleveland, OH, neighbors were able to piece together the activities that occurred in Mary Flynn's neighborhood on August 23, 1984. That afternoon, Apanovitch was doing work on a house across the street from Flynn's residence. He approached her and offered to paint her windowsills. Later that evening, at about 10 p.m., a neighbor saw Flynn walking from her car to the back door of her home.

The next morning, on August 24, Marty Flynn, Mary's brother, arrived at her home after she did not answer her phone. He found his sister lying face down on her bed, stabbed and beaten, with her wrists bound behind her back.

The pathologist later determined that Mary had been stabbed in the back of the neck, leaving tiny pieces of wood embedded deep inside the wound. Police had found that a piece of wood was missing from a windowsill in Mary's house. The pathologist also determined she had been killed between midnight and 6 a.m. and that semen was found on her body. This was collected during the autopsy, and several slides were created and stored for future reference.

The police searched her home and found a handwritten receipt for house painting, signed by Apanovitch, on her kitchen table. Mary Flynn's checkbook was also in the kitchen, with two canceled checks made out to Apanovitch for previous paintwork dated earlier.

Police looked into Apanovitch and found he had

served time for sexual battery and burglary. They also found he had been ejected from bars around town for fighting with other customers. Witnesses said Mary Flynn told them Apanovitch had made advances toward her, which she had rejected during the last time he painted for her. She reportedly told the witnesses she feared him.

Investigators questioned Apanovitch, and he could not reliably account for his whereabouts the night of Flynn's murder.

In November 1984, Anthony Apanovitch was tried for the murder of Mary Flynn.

During the trial, a detective testified that Apanovitch was seen leaving a neighborhood bar sometime around 9:30 p.m. and returned about 12:45 a.m. Witnesses at the bar said that, when he returned, he had a scratch on his face that hadn't been there before. According to the detective, Apanovitch allegedly asked the bar manager and waitresses at another bar, and a go-go dancer, to tell police that he had gotten the scratches in a fight outside. When questioned, the bar staff said they didn't even remember him being at the bar that night. According to the police, when Apanovitch was asked about the injury, he offered various disparate explanations.

A detective testified that a window at Flynn's home had been forced open, and part of the windowsill was missing. The prosecutor said that this was one of the windowsills that Apanovitch had offered to paint on August 23, and, according to the coroner, it was most likely the murder weapon.

In December 1984, Anthony Apanovitch was

convicted of rape, burglary, and murder. He was sentenced to death.

The slides from Mary Flynn's autopsy were located in the Cuyahoga County Coroner's Office in April 1991. Between November 2000 and September 2006, the Forensic Science Associates (FSA) DNA testing lab in California and the Cuyahoga County Coroner's Office tested DNA on the slides as part of their general practice of catching up on cases.

Authorities then asked Apanovitch to provide a DNA sample, but his attorneys objected on chain of custody grounds. In 2007, a federal district court ordered Apanovitch to provide a DNA sample for comparison, which was then sent to the FSA lab.

The lab found it was a match. A DNA match. The FSA report said that Apanovitch could not be excluded as the source of the sperm on one slide. The lab concluded that the chance that it belonged to another individual remained 1 in 285 million, which is more than double the male population of the entire U.S.

A defense expert acknowledged that the DNA *could* match Apanovitch. However, she questioned why Flynn's DNA profile wasn't more clearly found in the vaginal slide, and claimed that it appeared that other sources of DNA were found in the other samples.

In October 2014, a post-conviction hearing was held before Cuyahoga County Common Pleas Judge Robert McClelland that centered on DNA evidence on the vaginal slide. In February 2015, the judge acquitted Apanovitch only of the rape and vacated his guilty verdict and granted him a new trial. However, in November

2018, the Ohio Supreme Court reversed Judge McClelland's decision, holding that the trial court lacked jurisdiction. This ruling sent Apanovitch back to prison in November 2018.

Elana Wells had spoken to her father over the years and believed in him, but she had to admit that he could be both charming and manipulative, and that he was known to lie. She began to doubt his innocence after she learned about the DNA evidence against him.

Apanovitch had told his daughter that he never had sexual contact with Mary Flynn and that his sperm must have found its way onto the slide through an error in the lab. He had told her for years that DNA was always contaminated. He had told her he was opposed to DNA testing and had never supported it — until the defense chemist returned with the other DNA profiles.

According to Wells, one of the things that really shook her confidence in her father's innocence was reading about his past criminal history. She was able to obtain the transcripts of his previous trial, where he was found guilty of raping a 16-year-old girl in 1976. It turned out that that conviction was overturned on appeal because prosecutors in the trial had called his attorney as a witness, so he then pleaded guilty to the reduced charge of sexual battery. Elana Wells wonders why everyone had held up Apanovitch as a victim of the justice system while forgetting about what happened to Mary Flynn and her family.

It seems unprofessional for the defense DNA expert to de-emphasize the DNA match to Apanovitch and focus on the extraneous DNA. Is this a matter of presenting an opposing expert witness in an effort to confuse the jury?

It is interesting that all the innocence activists support the second DNA that excludes him but reject the first DNA that includes him, even stating that the DNA has exonerated Apanovitch from the crime. Most of the media articles and interviews with Apanovitch himself point to DNA clearing him, when, essentially, the DNA is a match to Apanovitch, establishing his guilt.

CHAPTER 21

TRUE CRIME LEADS TO THE INNOCENCE CRAZE

Although somewhat exploitative, many true crime TV shows exhibit a certain compassion towards the victims of crime. They show the detectives caring about the victims and working with the families to provide justice and some closure.

Do innocence advocates have this same compassion? Is that why they take on these cases even where a preponderance of the evidence points to the defendant's guilt?

In a world of true crime obsession, it seems easy for people to bury themselves in the rabbit hole of the Innocence Machine. They accept all the subtly biased language and campaign for the innocence of the imprisoned person. They may then fall into sketchy arguments and speculation about the case.

It seems to be a human trait that some people will always believe in some greater mystery, some police contrived conspiracy, that shows the innocent person was framed.

It then becomes easier to dismiss incriminating

evidence. It becomes easier to accept that any obscure anecdote can be used to add doubt to the prosecution's case.

People look for inconsistencies that suggest the defendant or convicted person is innocent. In real life, almost all criminal cases are subject to inconsistencies and extreme randomness.

New Witness Lacks Merit, Dog was Alive

In the second trial of David Temple for the murder of his wife, Belinda Temple, the defense said that they had new evidence and a new witness to prove that a 16-year-old neighbor was the real murderer. The defense claimed that the new evidence would prove David Temple's innocence.

On January 11, 1999, Belinda Temple was found dead in a bedroom closet in her home in Katy, TX. Belinda, who was seven months pregnant, had been shot in the back of the head by what appeared to be a 12-gauge shotgun.

It seemed to police that she had been shot sometime in the afternoon of the 11th because they had learned that when she had arrived home that afternoon her husband, David Temple, had left to go on errands. David told police he and their young son had gone to various locations around the city, and then, upon returning home, discovered the burglary of their home and his wife dead in their upstairs bedroom closet and called police.

Katy police almost immediately thought the burglary had been staged. The glass had been broken at the apparent point of entry at the back door, and it looked as if it had been broken after the door had already been opened. Drawers were pulled out, but nothing was disturbed. A television had only been moved slightly, and jewelry was left untouched. Nothing appeared to have been stolen from the residence.

Police also immediately noticed the Temple's dog barked at strangers, and in fact, because of the aggressive dog, responding officers were prevented from entering the backyard and the house until David moved the dog into the garage. The police also heard the dog barking while they were investigating and canvassing the neighborhood. One thing the neighbors said was that they had not heard the dog barking earlier that day.

The police eventually found out that David had been having an affair with another woman. When contacted, the woman, a fellow teacher at his school, said he had spent the New Year's holiday with her. Police learned that David had told everyone that he had gone hunting during that holiday weekend.

When questioned, David Temple said he didn't have a 12-gauge shotgun, but a hunting buddy came forward and said he did have one.

Crime scene investigators photographed and carefully examined the path of the broken glass from the possible entry door. The reason it appeared staged is that the glass indicated the door was open at the time of the break, and a hutch next to the door had items on top that had not been disturbed.

David Temple's timeline during the crime was then carefully investigated. They used store surveillance footage to determine the exact times he was in the stores. Temple said that he went directly to the store, but the police determined that his timeline was missing about 37 minutes when they put together his arrival at the stores he and his son had visited that day. For some reason, he had chosen stores far away from his home that day.

Police also found a witness who contradicted David's claim about the route he had taken that day. The witness stated he saw David at an intersection near a remote area of town, which coincidentally was an area where the Temples owned property. When police recreated the trip from that wooded area, it accounted for the time gap in his travels.

David Temple was arrested for the murder of Belinda Temple in November 2004. The trial began in October 2007.

During the trial, the defense proffered the theory that a 16-year-old neighbor had actually committed the crime. The prosecution, led by Kelly Seigler (*Cold Justice*), countered that the dog didn't bark that day, and there was no evidence that the boy was involved. The prosecution also presented all the other evidence gathered during the investigation, the timeline gap, the store surveillance videos, and the witness at the intersection near the Temple's property. On November 15, 2007, David Temple was found guilty of the murder of his pregnant wife, Belinda Temple.

During the next few years, Temple's lawyers advocated for his release, and in July 2015, David Temple won his appeal based on a Brady violation, that the prosecution withheld evidence, and other prosecutorial misconduct. Kelly Siegler had claimed that the prosecutor did not disclose important information in the case. An appeals court ruled 4-3 for a new trial based upon certain reports not being given to the defense. David Temple was released from prison, and the Texas prosecutor, Kelly Seigler, was denigrated in the innocence machine media.

In July 2019, David Temple's second trial began. The new prosecutor's case was similar to the one presented in the first trial. The evidence of staging, the lack of the dog barking, the videos from the stores, the timeline gap, the witness at the intersection who saw Temple in his truck that day, and the affair were all among the evidence presented during the second trial. They also brought in a glass expert to explain why the location of the glass was suspicious.

The defense then brought in the young neighbor, who was 16 years old at the time of the crime. He passionately denied being involved in the crime. He was a confident and believable witness. Then the defense brought in the new witness who claimed that the young neighbor boy had told him he was the person who murdered Belinda Temple.

Upon cross-examination by the prosecution, the new witness gave more details about what the then-16-year-old had told him. The new witness said he had told him that he had also shot the family's dog that day. This statement delegitimized the testimony of the new witness and new evidence. The dog had never been harmed, and the new defense witness was easily discredited.

In August 2019, David Temple was again found guilty of the murder of his wife, Belinda Temple. He was eventually sentenced to life in prison.

The Temple case is a good example of an innocence

activist using a new witness or new evidence to try to prove that a convicted person is innocent.

It appears that the innocence machine was at work in granting Temple a new trial. The justifications for a new trial were relatively thin. The considerable incriminating evidence is why Temple was convicted twice.

The terrible thing about innocent cases is that the defense does not have to play fairly. They can try almost anything to get a new trial for their defendant. They can bring in new fantastical scenarios and "new evidence" that doesn't exist or is impractical. The new evidence may not even be exculpatory, but if it wasn't presented at the original trial, it may convince a judge to grant the defendant's release and call for a new trial.

It is worth wondering why competent attorneys get involved in these cases. Does it mean that there is some substance to the defendant's innocence? Not necessarily. Is it to obtain a win by getting a new trial? Even if the defendant is judged guilty again?

Innocence Campaign Ignores DNA & Ballistics

Who could be a better advocate for a convicted person's innocence than Kim Kardashian? Kim Kardashian and Viola Davis advocated for Julius Jones when he was on death row in Oklahoma. Kardashian publicized his case through social media, tweeted on X, recruited other celebrities, and visited Jones in prison.

There is a slick, well-produced website, Justice for Julius Jones, that states it was "a racist trial and conviction." There are statements on other websites claiming that this was "a death penalty case of a black man accused of killing a rich white guy."

In 2018, the ABC show *20/20* aired an episode titled " The Last Defense – Julius Jones." A review said it was a "documentary series that explores and exposes flaws in the American justice system."

The Jones case received international attention due to the controversy promoted by innocence activists. However, the Oklahoma Court of Criminal Appeals (OCCA) reviewed the case and stated that there was "an "overwhelming" body of evidence consisting of "a co-defendant who directly implicated Jones, eyewitness identification, incriminating statements made by Jones after the crime, flight from police, damning physical evidence hidden in Jones' parents' home, and an interlocking web of other physical and testimonial evidence consistent with the State's theory."

On July 28, 1999, at around 9:30 p.m., Paul Howell, his older sister Megan Tobey, and Paul's two young daughters pulled into the driveway of Paul's parents' home in Edmond, Oklahoma. When Paul exited his GMC Suburban, he was approached by a black male with a gun who demanded that Paul give him the keys to the Suburban. Megan Toby heard a "pop" and quickly ushered the girls towards the house, yelling for help. Someone said something about "keys." She then heard a second gunshot and saw that her brother, Paul, had been shot in the head. Megan saw that the suspect wore a white T-shirt, a red bandana over his face, and a black cap. The carjacker then drove off in the Suburban.

The medical examiner would later determine that Paul Howell died of "a single contact wound," suggesting that the gun was pressed against his head when it was fired.

Edmond police responded to the scene and released information about the stolen vehicle. On July 30, the police located the Suburban south of Edmond in Oklahoma City, in a grocery store parking lot. They canvassed the area to see if anyone saw who left it in that parking lot and spoke with Kermit Lottie, who owned an auto body shop just blocks from where the vehicle was found.

Lottie told police that a man he barely knew, along with another stranger, offered to sell him the Suburban the day before, but he refused to buy it. Lottie provided the police with the man's, whom Lottie knew as "Day Day's," business card. On the card was the name Ladell King, along with his contact information.

Police questioned Ladell King, and King told them that on July 28, another man named Chris Jordan showed up at King's apartment, and then a few minutes later, a man named Julius Jones showed up driving a Suburban. King said Jones was wearing a red bandana, and the two men had come to see if King could help them sell the Suburban. King told police that the next day he found out the Suburban was linked with a murder, and he declined to help them sell it. King told police he had a number for Julius Jones, and they traced it to Jones' parents' house.

Police officers went to Jones' parents' house and, once outside, called the phone number; Julius Jones answered. The officer told Jones that police were outside the house and wanted to talk to him about Howell's murder. Jones then escaped from the home.

Warrants were obtained for Jones' arrest and for the search of his parents' home for evidence. In Jones' bedroom, detectives discovered a white T-shirt and a black stocking cap. They also found a Raven .25-caliber semiautomatic pistol wrapped in a red bandana that was hidden in the ceiling of the closet. Hidden behind the cover of the doorbell chime, officers discovered a .25-caliber magazine. The magazine held five bullets, and, if filled to capacity, it was missing two bullets. Ladell King had told police Jones had carried a gun of that type.

Within the next few days, Chris Jordan and Julius Jones were arrested.

When questioned by police, Jones said he had an alibi, that he was at home at the time of the murder. He said that his parents would confirm it. Jones said that Chris Jordan committed the homicide and carjacking, and Jordan must have planted the gun and red bandana in his bedroom two days after the murder. Jones' parents told the police Jones was indeed home that evening.

When looking into Jones, police suspected that on July 9, 1999, Julius Jones was the person who had robbed a jewelry store with a gun while wearing a red bandana over his face. They also suspected that, on July 21 and on July 22, Jones stole two different vehicles at gunpoint.

Julius Jones was put on trial in February 2002. During the trial, Ladell King and Chris Jordan testified against Jones. Chris Jordan, Jones' co-defendant, pleaded guilty and received a 30-year sentence with the agreement he would testify for the prosecution.

King testified that on February 15, he saw Jones park the stolen Suburban at his apartment complex in north-west Oklahoma City. King said that Jones was wearing a white T-shirt, a red bandana, and black cotton gloves. King testified that, the next day, he went with Jones to south Oklahoma City to see Kermit Lottie about buying the vehicle. King said he knew from past experience that Lottie did not want a stolen car driven into his shop, so they parked the vehicle near a store called Central Grocery. King also testified that Jones had admitted to the shooting, saying that Jones told him that the gun "just went off."

King's girlfriend and neighbor both testified that they saw Julius Jones standing next to the Suburban and talking to King during the crucial time frame.

Chris Jordan then testified that, on the day of the shooting, he and Jones went cruising around Oklahoma City in Jordan's car, looking for a Suburban, which they knew was easy to sell. After passing on several other Suburbans, they spotted Paul Howell's at a local Braum's ice cream shop. Jordan testified that they were going to rob Howell in the parking lot, but decided there were too many people there. Jordan said they followed the Suburban until it pulled into the driveway of a home. Jordan said that is when Julius Jones got out of his car to steal the Suburban at gunpoint. While Jordan was getting out of the car, he heard a gunshot, followed by another. Then Jordan said Jones got into the Suburban, and they drove away.

A ballistics expert testified that the bullet removed from Howell's head and a bullet fired into the dashboard of the Suburban were both fired from the handgun found in the ceiling of the closet in Jones' bedroom, and that the ammunition found in Jones' car, which police located at a transmission shop, was the same caliber.

Jones' girlfriend, Analiese Presley, testified Jones had told her prior to Howell's murder that he had a .25 caliber chrome semi-automatic pistol and that she had seen such a pistol in his possession in the summer of 1999.

The defense presented evidence questioning who wore the bandana, suggesting that Chris Jordan committed this crime alone, and claiming that witnesses were untrustworthy.

On February 25, the jury found Julius Jones guilty of first-degree murder, felon in possession of a firearm, and conspiracy to commit a felony. Jones was eventually sentenced to death.

Then came the appeals. In a typical defense attorney appeal case, they claim a laundry list of items to see if they stick. And in this case, Jones's lawyers alleged several points of appeal, most of which the Oklahoma Court of Criminal Appeals (OCCA) easily dismissed. However, some of them were carefully considered: Jones' lawyers alleged that the evidence, such as the gun and bandana obtained from his parents' home should have been suppressed, arguing that the information in the affidavit for the search warrant was insufficient to establish probable cause. His lawyers also disputed the forensic evidence, particularly the tool-mark evidence showing the recovered bullets were all fired from the same gun. After careful consideration, the OCCA dismissed these points.

The OCCA found that Jones was not unfairly prejudiced by non-police witnesses' use of the word "carjacking" instead of "robbery." And that the other evidence was considerable.

Jones' lawyers filed these objections in an application for post-conviction relief in 2005, which the OCCA denied in 2007.

In the intervening years, numerous appeals and hearings were held. In 2017, Jones' lawyers filed a post-conviction application seeking to have the red bandana tested for DNA. DNA was extracted from the bandana, and the sample was analyzed. A partial DNA profile was obtained, and the major component matched Jones. Christopher Jordan was excluded as the primary component of this profile.

Due to the celebrity interest, media attention, and the defendant's claim of innocence, the Attorney General of Oklahoma responded with a statement that there was overwhelming evidence of guilt."

Similarly, the Oklahoma County District Attorney David Prater wrote a letter to the parole board objecting to commutation (which reduces a criminal sentence) and accusing Jones and his attorneys of "*a coordinated and alarmingly successful campaign of misinformation, spurred by media frenzy, which is specifically targeted to manipulate and mislead the public through dissemination of half-truths and, frequently, outright lies,*" and discussing what he described as Jones' "*extensive criminal history, the evidence and testimony in the case, the new DNA evidence from the bandana, and reasons for doubting the alibi offered by Jones' family, as well as Littlejohn and Berry's claims to have heard Jones confess.*"

Despite these assertions, on November 18, 2021,

Governor Stitt commuted Jones' sentence to life without parole. However, Jones can never be eligible for further commutation or pardon as part of his clemency.

Did the innocence activists in this case have it right? This wasn't a situation with just one mistaken witness. Multiple witnesses saw Jones wearing the red bandana, numerous witnesses saw Jones near or driving the Suburban, and various witnesses saw Jones in possession of the gun.

The ballistic evidence was especially significant as it directly tied the murder of Paul Howell to a gun found in Jones' bedroom. It must have been a shock to these advocates when they learned that a gun from his home was the murder weapon, and the DNA evidence that they requested came straight back to Jones.

Upon objective review of the evidence, it is clear why the jury in this case, the Oklahoma County District Attorney, the OCCA, and the Attorney General of Oklahoma all found Julius Jones guilty.

Silly String, Inconsistencies and a Fingerprint

The Darlie Routier case is listed on the Innocence Project website.

A 911 call was placed to Rowlett, TX, police at 2:31 a.m. on June 6, 1996. The caller said someone had broken into her home and the intruder had stabbed two of her children. When police responded, they found the victim had a cut to her throat and arm, and six-year-old Devon and five-year-old Damon were both found dead with their throats cut.

Police noticed a window screen in the garage had been cut, possibly as a point of entry. They found little other disturbance to the house.

Police questioned the victim, Darlie Routier, who told them she had fallen asleep on the couch while watching television with her two sons and, when she awoke, she saw an intruder in her house. She said she confronted the man, and he dropped the knife and fled through the garage. Routier told police she picked up the large knife, which was from her kitchen, from the ground and chased him away. At that point, she realized she had been wounded and her children had been harmed, and she called 911.

Upon further questioning, and as Routier repeated her statement, investigators wondered why she had only awoken after the attack that severely wounded her and her sons. It seemed they had already been attacked and killed. Investigators also observed no blood drops in the purported exit route of the intruder through the garage. They also examined the windowsills in the garage and noticed the dust was undisturbed where an intruder would have had to climb in, and the soil outside in the flower bed showed no signs of disturbance.

A fingerprint was found on the windowsill. The police examined it, but they could not match it to anyone in the family.

A world-renowned fingerprint expert, Pat Wertheim, would later testify before an appeals court that he could not rule out Darlie Routier's right ring finger as the source of the print. What that means to a fingerprint expert is that there were several points of identity, fingerprint ridge characteristics, present in both the inked print taken from Routier's right ring finger and the latent print recovered from the windowsill. This is more significant than a simple statement of "could not rule out" or "could not exclude." It means there were no discernible differences, no unexplained ridge characteristics, and no fingerprint ridge structure that did not appear in both impressions. Therefore, the print could be the defendant's.

Fingerprints are such that even a tiny section of ridge structure — an ending ridge, a bifurcation, or a break in a continuous ridge — inconsistent between the two impressions would be exclusionary, and that person could be ruled out. If there had been any differences in the Routier case, she would have been excluded, but she was not.

{The author once testified in a civil trial where a defendant who was acquitted of the murder of a young boy was suing the government for police misconduct. The author testified he could not rule out the defendant because of similarities between the defendant's fingerprint impression and a latent impression on the victim's glasses. All other persons submitted were excluded. Therefore, the court ruled that the police had probable cause to arrest. The plaintiff lost the case.}

Investigating the scene of the crime, police found a bloody sock about 75 yards away from the house. Subsequent lab tests showed that blood from both sons were present on the sock. The sock was determined to belong to Routier's husband.

Police photographed Routier showing her wounds, one of which was close to her artery in her neck. However, she did not appear incapacitated to responding police. Routier was taken to the hospital and released.

Police learned that Darlie's husband, Darin, along with their youngest son, a seven-month-old, were upstairs and unharmed.

Then there was the infamous Silly String incident, where she was filmed at the boys' gravesites spraying Silly String, smiling broadly, and singing "Happy Birthday." This was shown on the local news. Police thought her flat affect was inappropriate after the violent loss of her children.

Authorities arrested Routier on June 18, 1996, and charged her with the death of her two sons.

Routier was put on trial for the murder of her son, Damon, in 1997. During the trial, the prosecution presented the evidence of the undisturbed windowsill and flowerbed, the bloody sock was from the home, and the knife was from her kitchen. They suggested that Routier's injuries were self-inflicted, that the crime scene had been staged, and that she killed her sons because of the family's financial problems. In February, the jury found her guilty of the murder of Damon and sentenced her to death. She was never tried for the death of her son Devon.

The media surrounding the case was immense, almost all of it resting on the premise that Darlie Routier was innocent. Several books and television shows have been made about the case, including *Forensic Files*, *48 Hours*, Investigation Discovery episodes, and a four-part ABC documentary.

A lot of the speculation on the part of innocence advocates has been centered around the thought: Why would a woman just up and kill her children? A counterthought is: Why would an intruder break into a home and kill the children?

Upon objective review of this case, there is no overwhelming incriminating evidence present as there is in many of the other cases. However, there are also no glaring misconceptions or evident missing proof that would allow the declaration of innocence.

It is essentially a matter of opinion whether Routier's injuries were severe enough to prevent her from planting the bloody sock and staging the crime. A lot of the support comes from empathy and thoughts that a woman could not brutally kill their own children, even though there are many historical cases where this very thing has happened.

One interesting aspect of the Darlie Routier case is that the defense attorneys requested a review of the fingerprints, which ultimately did not benefit her. The fingerprint on the windowsill was most likely hers, but there was not enough detail present for the fingerprint expert, one of the most respected experts in the field, to tie it to her. But it was also not the fingerprint of a mysterious attacker.

CHAPTER 22

THE CSI EFFECT

Another important factor, often in coordination with the reasons attorneys submit for exoneration, is the CSI effect. The CSI effect is the expectation that forensic evidence will be presented during a trial. The term is derived from TV shows such as *CSI: Crime Scene Investigation*, in which forensic evidence is always found at the crime scene depicted in the shows.

The CSI effect leads jurors to automatically expect the presence of fingerprints, DNA, and other extensive crime scene evidence. The CSI effect has a way of diluting other evidence and deeming old-fashioned circumstantial evidence as insufficient to reach a guilty verdict. This may even weaken technological evidence, such as cell phone records, GPS tracking, computer searches, and financial records. The CSI effect could hinder a case that had substantial circumstantial evidence uncovered through interviews, CCTV footage, wills, and insurance records.

In one highly publicized incident, the L.A. County District Attorney placed some of the blame for actor

Robert Blake's acquittal on the CSI effect. The DA noted that the "not guilty" verdict came despite two witness accounts of Blake's guilt, and he claimed that the jury members were "incredibly stupid."

In an article in the *National Institute of Justice*, "The 'CSI Effect': Does It Really Exist?" Judge Donald E. Shelton described one instance in which a jury member complained because the prosecution had not dusted the lawn for fingerprints, a procedure that is impossible and has not been demonstrated on any TV crime show. This is the CSI effect taken to the nth degree.

Then there is the TV effect. Criminals watch true crime shows on TV and know just what to do to prevent the leaving of forensic evidence.

This actually creates a vicious cycle where the criminal, after watching these shows, will know how not to leave evidence, use bleach for cleanup, burn bodies, or place bodies in water, or bury bodies so that decomposition will wipe away forensic evidence. And then, with the CSI effect, jurors who expect forensic evidence will have a difficult time deciding on guilt.

CHAPTER 23

A CELEBRITY IS ALWAYS INNOCENT

Is there a temptation to support seemingly innocent celebrities who are charged with a crime? Do people always accept that celebrities are innocent? Even of despicable crimes such as child molestation?

Because there is such a fine line between the consideration of guilt and innocence in people's minds, there seems to be a deference given to celebrities.

He Couldn't Be Guilty of Such a Horrible Crime

The Michael Jackson case always seemed to have two diametrically opposed sides. The country was divided about whether Michael Jackson was innocent of abusing young boys. Many people believe the mega pop star was totally innocent of any wrongdoing in the case that led to his 2005 trial. They believe none of the allegations against Jackson are valid and will forever think he is innocent.

Despite seven accusers, many of whom had received

monetary payments, including two accusers who received around 20 million dollars in a settlement, Jackson is considered by many innocent of any crimes, including inappropriate behavior. They argue that settlements could have been intended to prevent the accusers from sharing their stories with the media.

These payments were uncovered only through investigative reporting, leading to a *Financial Times* report.

The Los Angeles Police Department first began investigating Jackson in August 1993. This was based upon allegations that he possibly molested four different children.

Some of the allegations involved an unnamed child. According to a *Vanity Fair* article, the boy's mother questioned whether her son was sleeping in Jackson's bed. The family claimed the boy slept with Jackson every night for several months.

In September 1993, a lawsuit was filed against Jackson for inappropriate behavior with a family member's son, who initiated the lawsuit. It is believed that this lawsuit was settled out of court.

Also in 1993, the mother of a young Australian boy talked on CNN about his son staying in Jackson's room at night, but dismissed any inappropriate behavior.

Michael Jackson's sister, La Toya Jackson, came forward in December 1993 at a press conference in Israel to say that the allegations against her brother were factual.

In September 1994, Los Angeles prosecutors announced they would not pursue the case against Jackson due to the alleged victim's unwillingness to testify.

There were no further public accusations of Jackson

until a documentary was released. A significant point in the history of allegations against Michael Jackson was the premiere of the documentary *Living with Michael Jackson* in February 2003. In the film, British journalist Martin Bashir interviews Jackson and shows him with young boys around him, including Jackson holding hands with one of them.

In November 2003, Michael Jackson was arrested on child molestation charges. The case went to trial in February 2005 in Santa Maria, CA.

A number of celebrities testified on Jackson's behalf, including actors Macaulay Culkin and Chris Tucker and choreographer Wade Robson. The witnesses said they had slept in the same bed with Jackson but said he never acted inappropriately.

The primary victim, a boy who appeared in the Bashir documentary, testified at the trial that he'd had sleepovers at Jackson's home and that Jackson had acted inappropriately with him and made advances on him.

Martin Bashir testified, questioning the instances of an adult man sleeping in a bed with young children, and said he had asked Jackson about these occurrences and that Jackson told him there was nothing wrong with what they did.

The prosecution also presented testimony about past allegations against Jackson to make the point that Jackson had a propensity to commit such crimes. This testimony mentioned the 1993 case.

A person whose mother worked as a maid at Neverland Ranch testified that Jackson had abused him on several occasions. The defense brought out the fact that, like many of the Jackson accusers, he had at first denied the abuse.

Members of the Neverland Ranch staff testified that they had witnessed inappropriate behavior by Jackson on numerous occasions in the early 1990s. A former maid at the ranch testified that she had seen Jackson kissing boys on several occasions. The defense characterized the staff as coming forward for money.

One of the former housekeepers on the ranch said that the boys staying there would often remain in the bedroom with Jackson. She also said she never saw Jackson giving the boys alcohol.

Jackson's cook testified that he once came upon Jackson with his hand in a boy's underpants.

A flight attendant testified that she had seen Jackson put his arm around a boy while he was listening to music.

Two brothers who had spent time at the Neverland Ranch both testified that Jackson had acted inappropriately with them. The boys' mother also testified to the situation with her sons. The defense brought in past lawsuits of the family to discredit their testimony.

Janet Jackson also testified against her brother and said she was aware of Jackson's inappropriate behavior.

On June 13, 2005, the jury, after deliberating for around 32 hours, returned a verdict of not guilty. Michael Jackson was acquitted of all charges. It seems the jury did not believe all the witnesses, except those celebrities who testified in Jackson's favor, and could not accept Jackson was the monster the prosecution had portrayed him as.

On June 25, 2009, Michael Jackson died of a drug overdose.

In January 2020, the Jackson estate agreed to settle the lawsuit claims of several unnamed accusers.

Is our society set up in a way that celebrities are always innocent?

The Most Famous Celebrity Acquittal in History

The 1995 O. J. Simpson case probably had the most inculpatory and incriminating evidence in the history of criminal justice. His acquittal is also probably the most confusing acquittal in history.

Though many people were astounded by the verdict, after Simpson was acquitted, large crowds around the court cheered and displayed their "O. J. is Innocent" signs.

A private investigator, William Dear, wrote a book in 2012, *O. J. Is Innocent,*

And I Can Prove It, where he acknowledges that Simpson could have been at the crime scene, but that he was innocent of the actual murders.

In a book by F. Lee Bailey, part of O. J.'s "Dream Team" defense, published in 2021, *The Truth about the O. J. Simpson Trial: By the Architect of the Defense*, Bailey declares O. J. innocent.

Despite the constant review of O. J.'s case, many people still think he was innocent; after all, he was not convicted in the trial.

A further review of the evidence in the case is necessary here. Nicole Brown Simpson and Ron Goldman were found dead a little after midnight on June 13, 1994. They had both been slashed and stabbed to death in the courtyard just outside Nicole's condo, in Brentwood near Los Angeles, CA.

It was evident to LAPD investigators that a strong knife was used, and O. J. Simpson was known to have possessed one that was never found. A store owner remembered selling Simpson a large knife.

The slicing of the victim's throats was similar to that of a military-type attack. Simpson was given instructions on a similar military attack move for a movie prior to the murders.

A black knit cap was found at the crime scene, and the hair retrieved from the hat was consistent with Simson's head hair. The knit cap also had fibers similar to those found in Simpson's Bronco.

A pair of gloves was given to Simpson by Nicole, which were similar to the glove found at the crime scene. They were relatively expensive gloves. The glove had the victim's blood on it.

When questioned by police, Simson had a deep cut on his finger. He said he got the cut from a broken glass back in his hotel room. According to one of the detectives on the case, Simpson never asked what happened such as *How did Nicole die?*

LAPD had responded to the Simpson residence several times on domestic dispute calls. Nicole Brown Simpson had a safety deposit box with numerous photos of bruising on her body. One of the responding officers had been to the Simpson residence for one of those calls and knew where to take the detectives for a death notification.

On the night before the bodies were discovered, a limousine was scheduled to pick up Simpson and take him to the airport. While waiting, the limo driver saw someone in the porchlight about Simpson's size run into the front of the house. When he contacted Simpson over the intercom, Simpson replied that he had overslept. Kato, a friend of Simpson's living in a pool house apartment on the property, said there was no one else but him and possibly Simpson on the property at that time.

Kato told police that the house alarm could only be turned off at the front door of the Simpson residence. He didn't see anything but heard a loud bang on his back wall earlier in the night. He also did not know where Simpson was during the time of the murders.

This sound and entrance to the property would also explain how a bloody glove was dropped by the back fence behind Kato's apartment, which turned out to be a match to the one found at the crime scene. The glove would later be found to contain hair consistent with Nicole's hair and fibers consistent with Ron's jeans.

The alarm location would also explain why Simpson had to enter the property that way, travel past Kato's guest house, and down the driveway to the front door.

If the limo driver was at the front of the main gate, it would explain why Simpson had parked the Bronco by the back gate. It would also explain why Simpson had to jump over the back fence, hitting the back of Kato's apartment on the property and making the sound Kato heard about the time that turned out to be right after the murders.

Simpson's Bronco, parked by the back gate, had blood from numerous places within the interior of the SUV, including both the driver's and passenger's doors, and the steering wheel that was a match to both victims. A possible shoe print in blood was found on the passenger side floorboard and appeared to be size 12. Simpson wore size 12 shoes. There was also blood on the ground near the vehicle.

A blood trail that matched Simpson was found along the driveway from the rear of the property to the front door. Blood was also in the foyer of the residence, in the master bathroom, and on the master bedroom sink. Also, and significantly, the blood on the sock at the foot of Simpson's bed was a DNA match to the female victim.

As one can see there was not only circumstantial and situational evidence, there was an immense amount of direct evidence linking O. J. Simpson to the murders. The only way to make Simpson innocent is to discount all the blood evidence of his blood at the crime scene and the victim's blood on his car and at his home. Just creating the scenario that a racist cop dropped the glove doesn't explain away all the rest of the evidence. Just revealing all the mistakes that the LAPD made during the investigation doesn't discount the direct evidence in this case.

Is this an example that a celebrity is always innocent, no matter the evidence?

Celebrity Trumps Mounds of Evidence

Robert Blake was acquitted, but was he innocent of murdering Bonnie Lee Bakley on May 4, 2001? During Blake's trial, many protesters with "Blake is Innocent" signs marched outside the courthouse, and many people believed and continue to believe he is innocent.

On March 16, 2005, after a three-month-long criminal trial in Los Angeles Superior Court, Robert Blake was acquitted of the murder of his wife, Bonnie. After the judgment, according to the *Los Angeles Daily News*, several fans celebrated at Blake's favorite restaurant, the one that he visited just before the murder.

Robert Blake was a star who first appeared as a child in the *Our Gang/Little Rascals* short films. He eventually appeared in around 164 films, including *Of Mice and Men*, *Lost Highway*, directed by David Lynch, *Busting*, with Elliot Gould, and *Electro Glide in Blue*, with Clint Eastwood. He also starred in the movie *In Cold Blood*, based on Truman Capote's true crime novel, in which Blake played a murderer of a family in Kansas.

The details surrounding the murder of Bonnie Lee Bakley date back to the years before 2001. According to the two men who would testify at Blake's trial, he had asked two former stuntmen to kill his wife. One of the stuntmen asked Blake to buy a phone card so their calls couldn't be traced, and he directed him to where to buy one. Blake did just that. However, when the men had conversations, ostensibly about killing Bonnie Bakley, Blake called them from his own landline phone, which was traced to calls to the stuntmen. Police also found a receipt for the phone cards on Blake's desk. The calls continued until late in the afternoon of the day Bakley was killed.

One of the stuntmen testified that Blake drove him around while planning the murder and even took him by Vitello's in Studio City. The stuntman also said that Blake was to provide him with a weapon. He said that Blake showed him a .25 caliber handgun and said the gun was untraceable.

One of them also said that Blake told him about the house Bakley lived in. Blake told him the windows could pop out, and the former stuntman could go in and do it while she was asleep in bed. He also said Blake told him he liked the idea of doing it near Vitello's with her in his car, and that they discussed another plan to do it in the desert.

There was also a plan where Blake took his wife down the river near Bullhead City, where she could be shot on the beach, said one of the stuntmen. Coincidentally, Bonnie's sister (who did not testify in court) said Bonnie told her she and Blake were on the beach in Bullhead City one night, and Blake's friend/bodyguard ran up to him, with a gun in his hand, and said something like, "I can't do this." After Blake consoled his friend, they all went back to the hotel.

On May 4, 2001, Robert Blake and his wife, Bonnie Bakley, went out to dinner at Vitello's restaurant in Studio City, CA. In response to a 911 call from a neighbor, police found Bakley shot dead in the front passenger seat of Blake's car.

The car was parked about a block and a half from the restaurant, down a residential side street behind a large industrial renovation dumpster. The passenger door was open, and Bakley was inside leaning over. Police noticed that the window was about halfway down.

Blake told police that, after their meal at the restaurant, they walked down the street to his car. They got inside, and he put his keys in the ignition, rolled down the window, and realized he had forgotten his gun back at their restaurant table. He left the car to walk back up the block.

Blake said he returned to the restaurant to retrieve the weapon, went inside, found the .38 revolver, asked for a drink of water, and walked back to the car. When he returned, he found Bakley shot.

The restaurant manager said Blake usually parked right across the street, and that night, he didn't see Blake return to the restaurant. A busboy at the restaurant said he cleared the table but did not see the gun or see Blake return.

Days after the murder, the dumpster was thoroughly searched, and they found a vintage World War II German Walther pistol. The weapon was dirty from the material in the trash bin, but would eventually be matched ballistically to the 9mm bullets used to kill Bakley. The serial number was filed off, and it was not possible to determine the gun's owner.

In April 2002, Robert Blake was arrested and charged with Bakley's murder. Blake's friend/bodyguard was also arrested. When the friend's car was searched, police found a World War II vintage .9mm German handgun and a handwritten note in the form of a list that read: 2 shovels, small sledge, crowbar, 25 auto, get blank gun ready, old rugs, Duct tape-black, Drano, Pool Acid, Lye.

Blake's criminal trial for murder began on December 20, 2004, and lasted into 2005. The prosecution presented evidence from numerous witnesses, including restaurant staff, ballistic experts, law enforcement personnel, and crime scene investigators. A former LAPD detective also testified about a conversation he had with Blake, where he said if Bakley was pregnant and didn't get an abortion, "he was going to whack her."

The two former stuntmen testified about the plans Blake had to kill his wife, the calling cards, and phone contacts. However, the defense brought out that both men had difficulties with drugs, and insisted they could not be credible.

After the murder, Blake was eventually given a gunshot residue test and did have a small amount of gunshot residue on his hands. The defense contended that if Blake had used a gun, he should have had a large amount of gunshot residue on his hands. Therefore, he did not fire a gun that night. Police showed pictures of Blake at the scene, with his hands touching the grass, possibly also wiping his hands on his head and pants.

The prosecution presented the list from the friend's vehicle and said that it appeared like a murder to-do list to prepare for the murder. The defense claimed it was merely a shopping list for the friend/handyman to do work on Blake's behalf.

Robert Blake's alibi for the time of the murder is that he was back at the restaurant at the exact moment that Bonnie Bakley was killed.

On March 16, 2005, Robert Blake was found not guilty of murder. He was released to what was described as cheering crowds.

Robert Blake was a famous actor who many believed was innocent. He seemed like a Hollywood hero. Was it possible that the prosecution should have tried Blake for orchestrating the murder instead of actually pulling the trigger

In November 2005, in a civil trial, Robert Blake was found liable for intentionally causing Bonny Lee Bakley's death and was ordered to pay $30 million to Bakley's children.

Once again, Robert Blake's alibi for the time of the murder of his wife was that he was back at the restaurant, just a few yards away, at the exact moment that Bonnie Bakley was killed.

The claim that the list was a shopping list with those bizarre items is almost comical. The fact that Blake's friend/handyman had a WWII pistol and the murder weapon was a WWII pistol is a coincidence beyond coincidences. Lowering the windows of the car was also very convenient for the murderer that night.

Is Abuse a Factor for a New Trial

It was August 1989, José and Kitty Menendez were in the living room of their Beverly Hills, CA, home watching television, when someone came into their home and killed them with shotguns. Autopsies would later show that José was shot six times, including a shot to the back of his head. Kitty was shot 10 times, including a shot to her face in what seemed like she was crawling on the floor. The number of shots demonstrated that the assailant or assailants had reloaded their shotguns during the attack.

The Menendez's sons, Lyle and Erik, returned home to find the crime scene. Lyle called 911 and said someone had killed their parents. Lyle and Erik told the officers that they had not been at home and had just discovered their parents' bodies.

During the investigation, investigators learned that Lyle's friend, Glenn Stevens, remembered that one week after the killings, Lyle had suddenly gone back home from Princeton to destroy a new will from the family computer, and that he had gone home and erased it. Police also found that Lyle had contracted with a computer expert to get into the computer and ensure the file was entirely deleted.

In the months after the killings, police learned that the brothers spent hundreds of thousands of dollars on luxury items, businesses, and travel, including buying a restaurant, three Rolex watches, and a Porsche sports car. In a short time after the murders, the brother spent approximately $700,000.

Police questioned Erik's high school friend, who told them Erik had confessed to him that he had killed his parents. This friend also told them Erik had written a screenplay in where a son had killed his wealthy parents for their inheritance.

A girlfriend of Erik's psychologist came forward in 1990 to tell police that her boyfriend, the therapist, had told her that Erik had confessed to him during their sessions. She also told police that the psychologist had recorded the sessions.

Eventually, police learned that on August 18, 1989, just two days before the murders, Lyle and Erik went to several gun stores trying to purchase handguns. When they found out there was a two-week waiting period for handguns, they instead bought two 12-gauge shotguns along with boxes of ammunition.

Lyle Menendez was arrested in March 1990 in Beverly

Hills, and Erik Menendez turned himself in three days later after hearing he was wanted while he was in Israel. They were each charged with two counts of first-degree murder and held in jail awaiting their trial.

Each brother had a separate jury during their first trial, which started in 1993. The prosecution presented all the evidence described above. The defense presented many witnesses and claimed the brothers had been abused. Both juries became deadlocked on the first-degree charge, and mistrials were declared in January 1994 for both cases.

In a second trial, in 1996, the defense again presented the abuse charges. The prosecution presented the recorded therapy session tapes in which the brothers never mentioned being abused, though they did complain about their dictatorial father and mentally unstable mother.

Both Lyle and Erik Menendez were convicted of first-degree murder and sentenced to two consecutive life prison terms without the possibility of parole.

In May 2023, the brothers' lawyers requested a new hearing based on newly discovered evidence. A former Menudo member came forward with allegations of being abused by José Menendez when the band member was 14 years old. The appeal also included a letter written by Erik to his cousin in 1988, where Erik mentioned the abuse.

As of May 2026, Lyle and Erik Menendez remain incarcerated at the Richard J. Donovan Correctional Facility in San Diego after being denied parole in August 2025.

It is not even necessary to mention the extensive media coverage of this case. For example, there have been at least 11 documentaries, numerous movies, and multiple podcasts about the Menendez murders case. Several celebrities have also called for the brothers' release.

In this case, it is not a matter of innocence; the brothers have admitted they murdered their parents. It seems as if it is a question of whether they have served enough time if their father abused them. Should they be released with time served based on this factor?

CHAPTER 24

MISSTATEMENT OF THE VALUE OF EVIDENCE

There are often statements in cases listed on an archive/website in which innocence activists claim that the prosecution misstates or overstates the value of forensic evidence. This is even one of their listed categories or reasons for release or exoneration.

An example of the reverse.

On Nov. 27, 1995, a student at Maryland's Morgan State University, Terrence McKoy, was murdered after an attempted armed robbery at a bus station. The robber opened fire with his weapon, and a 10-year-old boy was also shot while passing by in a car.

A witness identified Kenneth Bond as the robber. Police found a bullet cartridge in Bond's home, and a firearms expert matched that cartridge to the bullet casing found at the crime scene.

Kenneth Bond was charged with the murder two years

later and sentenced to life in prison without the possibility of parole.

The Making An Exoneree website for Georgetown University's Prisons and Justice Initiative, an innocence activist website, states: "Kenneth Bond was convicted of murder on shaky eyewitness testimony and now-invalidated ballistics analysis."

A police sergeant for the Newark Police Department, Luke Laterza, is on video for a *Prisons and Justice Initiative* film promoting Bond's innocence. He states, "You cannot tell a casing came from a particular gun just by extractor marks; extractor marks are unreliable."

Gregory Laskowski, a retired Forensic Scientist with 39 years of experience, has a resume of Committee Chair on Sciences and Practices Committee, International Association for Identification, Oklahoma State University Adjunct Professor of Forensic Science at California State University, Bakersfield, and Johnson-Whyte Memorial Foundation Diamond Level Fellow.

Laskowski says, "Along with almost all of firearms and ballistic forensic scientists, I vehemently disagree with Mr. Laterza's statements and profess that firearms extractor comparisons are a valid scientific forensic technique. Being up to date with the field, I am unaware of any dispute regarding the comparison of extractor marks or any suggestion that they are unreliable. Unless, of course, those raised by defense attorneys, which is their job, I guess, to challenge evidence, but it definitely is not a discredited technique."

Kenneth Bond was released from prison after serving 27 years, his sentence reduced primarily due to his *rehabil-*

itation. Bond is trying for full exoneration. The Prisons and Justice website says, "His story became the center of a 2018 documentary and website created by Georgetown University undergraduates as part of the inaugural Making an Exoneree course, in which students reinvestigate decades-old cases and become advocates for people who have been wrongfully convicted."

If the release of Bond is based in any way upon the ballistic evidence being discredited, that is a misstatement of the value of evidence. And it is a wrongful release of a convicted person.

CHAPTER 25
NOT INNOCENT (AT ALL)

Some defendants protest their innocence with such confidence, persistence, and emotional force that they can appear credible to the public, the media, and even experienced advocates. Yet with a closer examination of the full case, including forensic evidence, witness statements, and corroborating details, it fully supports the original finding of guilt despite a defendant's ongoing declarations of innocence.

History of Criminality Contradicts His Innocence

The Rodney Reed case attracted international attention and celebrities, including Kim Kardashian, Beyoncé, Dr. Phil, Oprah, Gigi Hadid, Rihanna, and Meek Mill.

This case involved the 1996 murder of Stacey Stites. Stites was a 19-year-old woman living in Giddings, TX. Her body was found in some shrubbery behind a high school. An autopsy determined that Stites had been beaten, raped, and strangled with her belt. Her body was partially burned. Part of the belt was found near her body, and part near a truck belonging to her fiancé, who was a local police officer. They were scheduled to marry within three weeks of the murder.

Police suspected Rodney Reed due to the similarities to an attack on another woman. They located Reed who was already in jail from an investigation of an alleged rape of an intellectually disabled woman in 1995. Reed's DNA was on file, and when compared to the swabs taken from inside Stite's body, it was a match to Reed.

During an interview with police, Reed denied knowing Stites or having any relationship with her. At the trial, Reed's attorney elicited that Reed was having an affair with Stites but was trying to keep it secret. Prosecutors pointed out that Reed previously used this tactic in a prior rape trial in which he was acquitted.

Rodney Reed was convicted in May of 1998, and during the sentencing phase, the prosecution presented three women whom Reed had allegedly raped. Reed was sentenced to death.

In 2023, the Texas Court of Criminal Appeals denied Rodney Reed a chance for a new trial. The Appeals Court, in an extensive 129-page ruling, delved into every minute detail of the Reed case, analyzing all the prosecution's evidence and addressing the defense's proclamations regarding the case.

In part, the opinion states, "In May 1998, a Bastrop County jury found Rodney Reed guilty of the capital murder of nineteen-year-old Giddings resident Stacey Lee Stites. The indictment alleged that, in April 1996, Reed strangled Stacey to death in the course of committing or attempting to commit kidnapping and aggravated sexual assault. At the trial's punishment phase, the State introduced evidence linking Reed to five extraneous sexual assaults predating April 1996 and one attempted sexual assault in November 1996. Several of those assaults bore similarities to Stacey's murder. The jury answered the statutory special issues in favor of the death penalty, and the trial judge sentenced Reed to death."

The Texas Court of Criminal Appeals' opinion went on to strongly affirm the guilt of Rodney Reed in the 1998 murder case.

Despite all the machinations of the Innocence Machine and the support of endless celebrities, it still appears that Rodney Reed is being punished for committing this horrible crime.

Did the Innocence Machine lead to a misguided assumption?

The Free Moochie campaign evolved into a rap song called "Run Moochie Run." Moochie was on the run; he had escaped from a Broward County, FL, courtroom during a 2016 preliminary appearance.

A smart, innocent-looking, extremely personable young man, Dayonte Resiles, "Moochie," was arrested for the 2014 murder of Jil Halliburton Su, who was found stabbed 25 times and left in a bathtub.

When Moochie, 21, was arrested, rallies were held

under the "Free Moochie" sentiment, and a billboard appeared in the county. At the rallies, people wore "Free Moochie" T-shirts and protested for justice for young men like Moochie Resiles in the community.

Before, during, and after his trials, social media was blowing up in support for the Free Moochie campaign, and a Facebook account, "Justice for Dayonte Resiles," was opened. A billboard in Broward County read, "Two victims, one truth. Justice for Moochie. Who framed Moochie?"

When Resiles was brought into the Broward County court for a July 2016 pre-trial hearing, he slipped out of his shackles, shed his orange jumpsuit, and was seen fleeing down a stairwell. Apparently, a crew of about eight friends, fellow inmates, and his girlfriend had assisted in his escape, even providing him with a getaway car waiting outside the courthouse to whisk him away.

Video from the courthouse showed Resiles running across the courtroom, out a back door, and down the stairs. He was captured six days later at a Days Inn in West Palm Beach. His eight cohorts were eventually charged with helping Resiles flee the courthouse.

The "Free Moochie" movement continued. Eventually Resiles went to trial in 2021. The evidence pointed directly at Resiles as his DNA was found on a knife and a belt found at the crime scene. The defense challenged the DNA evidence, suggesting it could have been contaminated. Of course, everyone knows you can't contaminate DNA to become someone else's DNA.

After five days of deliberations, the jury announced they'd found him guilty of a lesser charge of manslaughter.

Nonetheless, when the judge polled the jurors on whether that was their verdict, the foreperson responded, "No." The foreperson said she didn't agree with the verdict of manslaughter. The juror thought the defendant should be guilty of murder. The judge had to declare a mistrial.

According to the foreperson, it was not a matter of innocence or guilt; the jury voted mostly for murder, as all felt the evidence was compelling, but a block of three members felt that "they did not want to send another young black man to life in prison." The foreperson said they felt pressured to render the lesser verdict.

Resiles was re-tried in 2022. The DNA from the knife and belt was again presented. The defense said that since the DNA was only found near the front door and not in the bedroom, the possibility existed that the defendant was in the home but did not commit the murder. The defense suggested someone else could have committed the murder, and since the police had originally concentrated on Su's son, he was likely the murderer. The defense also challenged the fact that DNA was not found on the knife that was recovered in water in the bathtub near the victim.

However, this time, the police investigation also submitted a sample from the point of entry on the back door, which matched Resiles' DNA.

Also presented was a phone call from the jail, on a recorded line, with Resiles asking a friend to lie and give him an alibi. Resiles also asked another friend to say that he had a cut, and that was why his blood was at the scene. The problem with this request by Resiles was that the DNA found at the murder scene was not in blood.

The jury in the second trial in 2022 found Resiles

guilty of first-degree murder, and he was sentenced to life in prison.

The Free Moochie case is a captivating lesson that no matter how much a community wants to will the innocence of a defendant, the innocence machine cannot always override compelling evidence of guilt.

CHAPTER 26

ESSENTIALLY GUILTY 42 PERCENT OF THE TIME

In my innocence movement research, I found a concerning statistic: In a little less than half the cases that the Innocence Project takes on, the clients' guilt is reconfirmed by DNA testing. In other words, of all the cases carefully vetted by the Innocence Project, 42% were confirmed guilty.

On the original Innocence Project website, innocence project.org:

"How often do DNA tests prove innocence in your cases? Does testing ever prove guilt?

"Among our cases that go to DNA testing, the DNA proves our client's innocence about as often as it suggests they are guilty. In a review of Innocence Project cases that went to DNA testing and were then closed over a five-year period, DNA testing proved innocence in about 43% of cases, confirmed the prosecution theory in about 42% of cases, and was inconclusive or not probative in about 15% of cases."

The Temple Sinai, Summit, N.J. informational website states that "The Innocence Project, … works to exonerate wrongly convicted via DNA testing and works to reform the criminal justice system to prevent future injustices. As of Jan[uary] 2020, the Innocence Project documented 365 DNA exonerations in the US. Twenty-one of these had previously been sentenced to death. Of all the cases taken on by the Innocence Project, about 43% of the clients have been proven innocent and 42% were proven guilty; the rest were inconclusive and not probative."

The Innocence Project states, "All potential clients go through an extensive screening process to determine whether or not they are likely to be innocent." If they pass the process, the Innocence Project takes up their case. Thousands of prisoners contact the Innocence Project each year. The Project then evaluates the cases for potential wrongful convictions.

The possible conclusions that can be drawn from this statistic are significant. Many of the cases they decide to pursue, based on the belief that the convicted person is innocent, result in the person actually being proven guilty. It also means that about half of the cases that seem to concern a wrongly convicted person are ultimately released or exonerated.

Both this category of cases and the number of cases in which the exonerated went on to commit crimes are important in the scheme of things. The good news is that true innocence organizations, such as the Innocence Project, seem to be very selective about the cases they decide are worth the time and money to appeal.

Does this mean that the concern of innocence activists is vastly inflated and hyperbolic?

Does it mean that due to the unstoppable Innocence Machine examining many, many cases for a thread of innocence, guilty people are consistently being released from prison?

CHAPTER 27

TECHNICALITIES AND MORE MISSTATEMENTS OF EVIDENCE

There appears to be an obsession with technicalities in many of the cases highlighted on innocence organization websites. This also becomes apparent in appellate court filings. Technicalities can be an easy avenue for appeals to gain new trials or the release of the convicted person.

Fitbit Case, One Misstatement Does Not Make Him Innocent

When Ellington, CT, police responded to a home on Dec. 23, 2015, Richard Dabate told them he believed an intruder might still be inside. Dabate was in the basement of the home, had one hand zip-tied to a chair, and had cuts on his body. Dabate's wife, Connie Dabate, was found shot dead on the basement floor. The gun on the basement floor was thought to belong to Richard.

Dabate told police that a masked intruder broke into their home, used zip-ties to tie him up, tortured him with a blowtorch, and stabbed him with a boxcutter. Dabate said he struggled with the intruder over the gun, and the intruder ran out of the home. Dabate said this was at about 9 a.m.

Police might have been a little suspicious since Richard had only been loosely tied to the chair, and his wounds were minor. They collected cell phones, computers, and alarm logs.

Eventually, police obtained the data from Connie Dabate's Fitbit watch. Data from the device showed that Connie had been moving around nearly an hour after Richard said that she had been killed. The Fitbit showed movement inside the house at 9:23 a.m., and her phone indicated she had been on Facebook between 9:40 and 9:46 a.m. A movement distance on the Fitbit starting at 9:18 a.m. was recorded for 1,217 feet. This is approximately the same as the distance from her car in the driveway to the home's basement.

During the investigation of the crime scene, police had a K-9 dog search the house to track the intruder. Instead of following a trail from the house, the dog seemed to alert on Dabate, who was in an ambulance being treated for his injuries.

Police learned that Richard was having an affair with a woman who was pregnant with his child. They also discovered from Dabate's phone a number of texts between him and the woman, including one on December 22 that said he would see her the next day.

On May 10, 2022, Richard Dabate was convicted of three charges — murder, tampering with evidence, and making false statements to authorities — and sentenced to 65 years in prison.

The basis for the October 2024 appeal stating that Richard should be given a new trial is that the prosecution asked him, "Did you feel like a ticking time bomb?" along with other statements the prosecutor made during the trial.

According to CBS CT News, the prosecution replied, "I don't think there's anything improper at all about using the defendant's own words, from a prior inconsistent statement, to impeach his testimony once he testifies."

In a March 2025 decision, the Connecticut Supreme Court gave its opinion on the Richard Dabate appeal. The opinion said that, despite finding improprieties by the prosecution, they were upholding the murder conviction. According to CBS News, the court suggested that the jury would have had to be unintelligent or lazy to agree with the defense's theory of the case. The justices said the state's case was very strong, and the prosecutor's missteps did not overshadow testimony by the 130 witnesses and 600 exhibits presented during the five-week trial.

This case falls into the category of "oh so close" — the appeal by the defense came very close to releasing a murderer back into society.

WHAT IS GOOD FOR THE GOOSE IS *NOT* GOOD FOR THE GANDER

It seems to be perfectly acceptable for a defense attorney, when speaking to the jury, to use a lot of linguistic techniques and descriptions to minimize some evidence, emphasize others, and dismiss some incriminating evidence entirely, but it is not acceptable for an expert witness to testify technically correctly if it might mislead the jury. It is also all right for a defense "expert" to provide an opposing conclusion to that of the prosecution's expert, but it is not proper for a forensic expert to testify if they might mislead the court.

In many cases on the Exoneration Registry, defense attorneys called over several years for evidence to be tested for DNA. In some cases, testing was conducted, but upon completion, it did not exonerate the defendant. In such instances, the defense may claim that the testing was not done properly, there was contamination, or it should have been performed by a private laboratory. Other factors are then used to try to obtain the person's release or a new trial.

Inadequate Legal Defense

The Charlie Dunn case is listed on the National Registry for Exonerations, but shouldn't be listed as a case of innocence. Many cases in the Registry exoneration chart list a release due to several reasons, such as inadequate legal defense; however, the convicted person was not actually declared innocent.

On June 27, 1987, Joyce Watkins, 39, and her boyfriend, Charlie Dunn, 43, brought Watkins' niece to Nashville Memorial Hospital in Nashville, TN. The four-year-old little girl had suffered head trauma, and the next day she died.

An autopsy revealed the girl's injuries had occurred during the time she was in the care of Watkins and Dunn, and both were charged with murder.

During the trial, the medical examiner described nine blows to the child's head. He said he thought that the injuries had occurred 12-14 hours prior to the death. A representative of the Kentucky Department of Social Services had received a complaint that the child in Watkins' care had welts on her body, and that Watkins had made a false statement about where the child was staying at times, and that she had taken her to a doctor. Other witnesses testified that they had seen the little girl with injuries over several medical incidents.

On August 5, 1988, the jury convicted Watkins and Dunn of first-degree murder. They were sentenced to life in prison.

In 2015, Charlie Dunn and Joyce Watkins were granted parole through the parole system. However, Dunn had already died in prison in January 2015. Watkins was released on parole in October 2015. According to the Registry of Exonerations, on January 6, 2022, Davidson County Criminal Court Judge vacated the convictions and ordered a new trial due to inadequate legal representation.

Gets a New Trial on Police Misconduct

The Eric Smokes case involves the release of a convicted person based on a technicality. The original case was brought to the attention of the New York County Conviction Integrity Unit.

It was New Year's Day 1987, and Jean Casse was visiting New York with his wife as tourists from France. He was mugged and beaten while walking along West

52nd Street in Manhattan. Casse was 71 years old and was taken to New York's St. Luke's-Roosevelt Hospital.

The French couple had been walking toward Times Square, and the attack occurred outside a restaurant. The head waiter at the restaurant told NYPD officers that he saw Jean Casse being attacked as he was on the ground, being hit by three or four young Black men. He described two of the men and their attire. The waiter also said he saw the smaller man go through the tourist's pockets and take his wallet.

Two other people witnessed part of the attack as they walked along West 52nd Street. One of the witnesses said that she did not get a good look at the main assailant's face but did describe him as a skinny Black male. Both witnesses said that Black male was about 6'1" or 6'2".

In the days prior to the New Year, police had been responding to calls and complaints about young Black men attacking and robbing people around Times Square. And on January 2, police arrested a 16-year-old named Jame Walker during an attempted robbery. When interviewed, Walker told NYPD investigators he had talked to a man named Eric Smokes, and Smokes said he had killed someone. In the interview with investigators, Walker described a method of robbery that Smokes had used, and it appeared to police to match the attack on Casse.

Smokes, 19, admitted he was in the area with his 16-year-old friend, but said that he did not attack Casse. Five teenage witnesses identified Smokes and Warren as the ones who assaulted and robbed Casse.

The Post-Conviction Justice Unit of the Manhattan District Attorney's Office (PCJU) moved to exonerate the two men after an investigation with defense counsel found the police had grilled the teenage witnesses who testified at trial. The teenage witnesses were deemed unreliable. They also found that the prosecution withheld other information about the witnesses from the defense.

In response to the PCJU report, the prosecution said it did not agree with everything in the defense motion but would not oppose the move to vacate and dismiss the charges against Smokes and Warren.

A New York State Supreme Court Justice granted the motion for a new trial and dismissed the original charges in January 2024. In the order, the justice included the new information obtained and the tactics employed by the police during questioning of the witnesses in his decision, stating that the case against Smokes warranted a new trial. However, the Manhattan District Attorney vacated both their convictions. Police misconduct led to this result.

CHAPTER 28
TIMING AND THE TIME FACTOR

While it cannot be proven, some cases taken up by the Innocence Machine may be based on the fact that so much time has passed that the original witnesses may no longer be available, evidence may be missing or degraded, and the prosecution has no desire to pursue such an old case.

Time Becomes a Factor in Retrial

A University Park, Texas, police officer responded on April 9, 1983, to a shooting in a neighborhood. Upon arriving, the officer found a man, James Sewell, gagged, handcuffed, and covered with blood, standing outside his duplex.

Sewell, who was known to police as a drug dealer, said that Billy Allen and two other men had shot him. Sewell was put in an ambulance, and the paramedics would later say that Sewell said, about five times, that it was Billy Allen who had shot him.

University Park officers searched the house, and in the

carport, they found Raven Dannelle Lashbrook dead in a car. The police processed the vehicle for fingerprints and found a palm print on the roof.

Using the name Sewell had given them, they found a Billy Frederick Allen who had a record of violent crimes and drug convictions. They obtained fingerprints on file for Billy Allen and were able to make an identification of the palm print on the vehicle that contained Lashbrook's body. Allen was arrested in California in April 1983, and in June, Sewell died from his injuries. Allen was charged with the murder and was put on trial in September 1983.

DURING THE TRIAL, THE DEFENSE PRESENTED testimony that Allen knew Sewell and that they had met prior to the murder, and Allen had put his hand on Sewell's vehicle. Allen was convicted of both murders on September 14, 1983, and sentenced to life in prison.

In May 2004, Allen's attorneys filed their fourth petition, raising inadequate legal defense and factual innocence. The appeal went forward, and in February 2009, the Texas Court of Criminal Appeals set aside the conviction and ordered a new trial.

In 2011, the Dallas County District Attorney dismissed the charges, saying that some of the evidence in the case had been destroyed by then, one witness had since died, and another had stopped cooperating. The prosecution would not retry Allen but declined to say he was innocent. Billy Allen was then released, but too much time has passed since the original case to retry him. Could this become a tactic of the Innocence Machine?

Time is a factor after Witnesses are Dead

On April 13, 1993, Mark Broxton was shot four times outside a store in New Orleans, Louisiana. After being shot, Broxton staggered into the convenience store and collapsed.

When New Orleans Police officers arrived at the scene, they found Broxton on the floor of the store. He was still alive and said he did not know who shot him. Broxton died later while being treated at a local hospital.

A man named Eric Price came forward and said he saw the shooting when he was standing on the other side of the street. He described the assailant as a Black male wearing a black, blue, and purple jacket and then discarding the jacket in a nearby dumpster toward the back of the store. New Orleans Police located the jacket and found a stamp in the pocket. The stamp was eventually processed, and a partial fingerprint was recovered.

During interviews with Broxton's friends, the police learned that 20-year-old Kuantau Reeder was a possible suspect. A woman also came forward to the police and told them that Reeder had told her he had committed the crime.

A police detective arranged a photo array, including Reeder, and showed it to Price. Price identified Reeder as the shooter and signed the back of the sixth photo, confirming his selection.

Police arrested Reeder in August 1993 and charged him with second-degree murder. Reeder went to trial in 1994, ending in a mistrial with a hung jury. His second trial occurred in 1995.

In the 1995 trial, Price testified to what he saw that day and said it was Reeder who did the shooting. The cashier at the store had testified in the first trial and said that he knew Reeder as a regular but did not see him that day; he could not be found for the second trial.

Reeder's testimony from the first trial was entered into the record. He said that he knew Broxton but did not shoot him. He said he was playing basketball nearby and had heard the shots. He also admitted to two prior convictions for drug possession and distribution.

The woman who came forward to say Reeder admitted to the killing testified that he really never said he did, but that she had heard rumors that he shot Broxton because of an argument between the two men.

The 1995 jury convicted Reeder of second-degree murder, and he later received a sentence of life without parole.

Reeder's defense attorneys brought forward several appeals.

In October 2021, the New Orleans Police Department examined the print from the stamp. The examiners assessed the print as unusable for identification purposes but could still exclude contributors. Reeder was compared and excluded.

At a hearing before a judge of the Orleans Parish District Court, the court ruled that the prosecutor was materially misleading in presenting the evidence. In December 2021, the judge vacated Reeder's conviction and dismissed the charge. Reeder was soon released from prison.

The prosecution said that a retrial was unfair and

impossible because two of the major witnesses, Price and the woman who testified about Reeder, were dead.

While some of the witness testimony in this case is suspect, the fact that so much time had passed and that the principal prosecution witnesses were deceased does not make Reeder innocent of this crime.

Sometimes Everybody is Wrong

In 2008, in a small town in Alabama, "Truth for Kerri" signs were displayed on almost every lawn. Townspeople held yard sales and fundraisers to raise money for Kerri Willoughby's defense. A website promoted a "Truth for Kerri" movement in support of her innocence and claimed that the truth would ultimately exonerate her. Kerri gave out autographed pictures of herself.

On April 22, 2008, Billy "Junior" Shaw, age 65, was found dead in his home in the Cartersville community, north of Ider, a small town East of Huntsville, AL. He was found by his stepdaughter, Kerri Willoughby, who called 911 after finding him slouched over in a chair in his living room. Kerri said she had given her stepfather CPR, and paramedics confirmed the death. Since the death was unattended by a physician, police arrived and took photographs of Shaw. Police initially thought that Junior had died of a heart attack. Then the police noticed that he had puncture marks, similar to medical injections, on both forearms.

Police were suspicious and suspected possible foul play, that perhaps someone had administered something to cause the death. A coroner also responded, and due to the unusual puncture marks, police requested that blood and urine be taken from the body.

No one in the family knew anything about the puncture marks, and, initially, the owner of the local funeral home, Kerri Willoughby's sister's husband, was suspected of causing the death. When first questioned about the marks, Kerri told police that she thought Junior had just had a doctor's appointment. Police checked with local doctors, and he had not been to one recently.

When police talked to Willoughby again, she told police she thought it was suicide because they had just lost her mother, Junior's wife, a short time before. Kerri even wrote a posthumous letter to him, wondering why he did that to himself.

Willoughby's sister began wondering about what had happened when Willoughby told her at a football game that she had taken some drugs to Junior to use on a bull that needed to be taken care of. Eventually, Willoughby told police that she had taken a drug called propofol to her stepfather for him to use on a bull he was having trouble with.

Police then directed the testing lab to test for the drug, and the results of the blood tests showed a presence of propofol. Kerri Willoughby, 32, then became the focus of the police investigation into Shaw's death.

The town rallied around Kerri Willoughby, proclaiming her innocence. Willoughby, a mother of two young children, maintained her innocence and had supporters numbering more than 1,300, who had joined her Facebook page, "Truth for Karri."

In May 2009, Junior Shaw's body was exhumed, and

an autopsy was performed. The Alabama Department of Forensic Sciences in Huntsville determined Junior died of a lethal injection of propofol, the same drug that killed pop star Michael Jackson. They also found the presence of vecuronium, a drug that causes muscle paralysis. Additionally, the autopsy showed bruises on Junior's wrists but none on his chest, which would usually be the case if he had been given CPR.

Investigators determined Willoughby most likely took the supply of propofol and vecuronium from Chattanooga Surgery Center, where she worked as a nurse until 2009. She had been a training nurse who trained others on how to use those drugs. At the time she worked there she was the sole custodian of the box that contained the drugs that were found in Junior Shaw. They also concluded that if Junior had given the drugs to himself, they would have been able to locate the vial and the syringe in the home.

Willoughby was indicted on a charge of capital murder in May 2010. Almost everyone in the community believed that this churchgoing woman, who helped others in the community, could not have committed this crime.

Even though Willoughby had been arrested and was in jail pending her trial, it seemed that almost everyone in town still believed she was innocent. She gave autographs, and in one signed photo, she mentioned that Angelina Jolie might portray her in the movie.

Investigators learned that Willoughby had been operating as a business manager for the Shaw's saddle business, and the prosecution found out that, prior to her death, Kerri's mother, Lila Shaw, had become aware of several banking inconsistencies and inappropriate use of business funds. Junior Shaw also became aware of the banking issues. He closed one business account that Willoughby had access to and opened another account, removing Willoughby from the company on April 1, 2008. That same day, Lila Shaw, Kerri's mother, died in a fall at the Shaw residence.

They then learned that the next day, Willoughby attempted to cash a $2,000 check at a teller window at the Bank of Dade, which was signed by Lila Shaw. It seems the teller knew Kerri and that Lila Shaw had just died the day before. The teller called Junior Shaw to authorize the check, and Shaw did not approve it.

Prosecutors contacted a medical expert, who prepared a report for trial. The report made several key points about the case. The expert pointed out that it would be difficult for an untrained individual to fill a syringe with propofol and that Mr. Shaw would not be able to administer an intravenous injection with the opposite hand. The expert also suggested that Junior would have been unconscious within one minute following the injection of the propofol. And because of the level of propofol present in Shaw's urine, they concluded that Shaw was alive at the time it was administered.

Prosecutors also addressed the suggestion that the drugs were taken to subdue a bull; they said there was no bull. They also said that Junior had been active in the days prior to his death, and the family said he was not suicidal.

On February 8, 2012, the DeKalb County courtroom was filled with supporters of Kerri Willoughby and local media. The jury had been seated, and the trial was ready to proceed. Then, unexpectedly, Kerri turned around and said, "I'm sorry" to the crowd. Shocking those in the audience, she admitted she gave Billy Junior Shaw the injections, she knew it would kill him, she thought she would inherit money, and she feared being exposed for her theft of funds. Willoughby pleaded guilty to a lesser charge of murder and was sentenced to 20 years in prison.

Eventually, authorities found out that Willoughby had written many letters while she was incarcerated prior to the trial. She had written a love letter to another person in the DeKalb County Jail, as well as a love letter to an unknown person who was also incarcerated.

Some letters went to another inmate, one of her apparent love interests in the DeKalb County Jail, who was a man who had pleaded guilty to the December 2009 killing of his estranged wife.

The text of some of the letters she sent to others included her thoughts on plans for a "beach wedding," "making love every night," and "bringing our families together." She also wrote, "I want to be your wife," and said in the letter. "I love you, I'm in love with you. Doesn't that matter to you? I've already sent you two other letters with no response."

In a letter to the convicted murderer, she wrote, "I trust you and your judgment, and I'm looking to you as the head of our household now and will follow your counsel. You and God are my strong towers, baby."

One of the letters she wrote to another person was extremely graphic and explicit.

Kerri also wrote to her husband, Jason: "I want to win this trial, and I should win it because I'm innocent, but I don't think it's going to go my way." She said in her letter:

"Billy is going to lie. Kim is going to say I stole my mother's identity. Nancy is going to say mother was upset at the bank. I signed out the drugs that were in his system. I have no alibi, and who is going to believe I was really taking a nap on the side of the interstate? Plus, I have two bankruptcies before I was 30, and now this sex letter. Let's face it, it doesn't look good..."

Then Kerri Willoughby admitted to her crime in court, showing her supporters that they were all mistaken about her innocence. The best appraisal of this case comes from Willoughby's words in the letter she wrote to her husband: "It doesn't look good."

Even after her admission in court, there were still people who professed her innocence and pointed to possible motives for her crimes, such as the possibility that she was suffering from PTSD after domestic abuse.

If Kerri Willoughby hadn't confessed, would this have been a case for an innocence movement? Would all the people calling for her innocence have caused a groundswell of support from more people in Alabama and more supporters around the country? Would it have led to her being released from prison?

CHAPTER 29

LIES, LIES, AND DAMN LIES

Though this phrase is probably a result of the Mandela Effect, lies are a component of the Innocence Machine, through and through. The Mandela Effect is the concept that many people remember something that happened, but in reality, it didn't happen, such as the premature death of Nelson Mandela or the Monopoly man wearing a monocle.

Along with the maxim that everybody in prison says that they're innocent, there could be an axiom that those who say they're innocent are liars.

Lying can be categorized in two main ways. To conceal or to falsify. In concealing, it is the withholding of information, the spin of the information, or the presentation of alternate facts to change the situation. This concealing is the absence of incriminating evidence when describing a case, such as "No tangible evidence of his guilt." "Out of all of the witnesses, the only hard evidence was one witness and his cell phone records."

Falsifying is presenting information as if it were true. "The defendant was wrongfully convicted." "He was wrongly imprisoned." "He was unjustly incarcerated." "The detectives doggedly pursued a wrongful conviction."

A consistent thread throughout these cases is the defendants' prevarications. In fact, it is baffling that their lies are not considered a major factor in determining whether they are innocent. It is equally perplexing why appellate courts and judges don't consider defendants' untruths a significant factor in their decision-making.

Another baffling segment of these prevarications that fits the concealing portion is the contribution of appellate attorneys who bring these cases forward. For example, in the Corbett case described further in this section, the appeal was based on what seems like two legitimate pieces of evidence: the original interviews with the children and new evidence from audio recordings that seem to demonstrate verbal abuse by Corbett. However, the children in the original interview recanted, and the audio recording was done in secret and could easily have been set up. It could have also captured the killing, but that was not available.

The case involving the killing of Jason Corbett is all about lies, from start to finish.

After a multifaceted investigation, Molly Corbett and Thomas Martens, Molly's father and a retired FBI agent, were convicted of second-degree murder in 2017. A defense team appealed the convictions, and they were released in 2021, awaiting a new trial. After they were recharged, they pleaded to the lesser charge of voluntary manslaughter in 2023. They were both released in June 2024 after spending only a few additional months in prison.

Before we discuss the Corbett case, a review of other cases and the defendants' lies can be enlightening. The prevarications and falsehoods in all these cases can be verified with facts, so they are not speculation.

It is not known why a defendant's lies are somehow accepted and not used as a primary point of guilt in these cases. They certainly should have been in the Corbett case. First, here are the other cases with fact-checked lies.

In almost every case, without fail, the defendants in the following incidents lied when initially questioned, mostly about their whereabouts at the time of the murder, many about their relationship with the victim, and some about the actions that occurred during the incident.

In a case not featured here, there were so many lies that Casey Anthony told that it was difficult to count. Like her fictional nanny, Zanny, where Zanny lived, where Casey worked, for how long, a boyfriend, and more. So much so that it would have been hard to take her seriously about anything.

One has to consider the lies told by defendants when they think that these people may be innocent. Why are they lying? It doesn't seem sufficient to give the cursory reasons that they were hiding an affair, or they were embarrassed about revealing something. These defendants' lies have a purpose, and most of the time, they are meant to protect themselves and cover up their crimes.

For example, Adnan Syed lied about his whereabouts the day of Hae Min Lee's murder, which was contradicted by his cell phone records. Syed also lied about asking for a ride that day and about his car needing repair.

Caitlin Conley lied about the poison in her boyfriend Adam Yoder's car and about the fake e-mail account she had made to deflect attention away from her.

Dana Chandler lied about going to Rocky Mountain National Park during the time Mike Sisco was killed. When confronted with a video taken at the park, she said she slept in her car somewhere.

After driving from California to Salt Lake City, getting lost on I-15, and supposedly bypassing Arizona, Jody Arias first said she was not at the Mesa murder scene of Travis Alexander, then changed her statement and said two masked men committed the crime, then said she killed her ex-boyfriend in self-defense.

Scott Peterson lied about his affair and about the circumstances of his wife Lacey's life insurance.

Julius Jones told falsehoods about how the gun was hidden in his room, his whereabouts, and who he was with on the day of the murder of Paul Howell

Robert Roberson lied about how his child, Nikki, received those horrific injuries.

David Temple lied about his affair, owning a 12-gauge shotgun, and his route on the day of the murder of his wife, Belinda Temple.

In the Kenneth Bond case for the murder of Terrence McKoy, the campaign deceptively claimed that the firearms examination technique had been discredited.

Marcellus Williams, or at least his campaign, misrepresented that DNA exonerated him from killing Felicia Gayle.

It seems that Richard Dabate lied about everything that happened that morning when he was attacked and tied to the chair in the basement, as proven by the data on his wife Connie's Fitbit.

Carrie Willoughby lied to everybody but finally had to come clean and turn around to say, "I'm sorry," to her supporters in the killing of her father, Billy "Junior" Shaw.

Alex Murdoch was deceitful about not being at the hunting lodge that evening until the phone video proved he was there just before his wife, Maggie, and son, Paul, were shot and killed.

Maurice Caldwell and Anthony Porter orchestrated grand conspiracies from their jail cells with false information regarding the murders of Judy Acosta by Caldwell and Marilyn Green and Jerry Hillard by Porter.

The Innocence Machine tends to discount the defendant's lies wholesale when they should be a primary consideration in most cases of potential innocence. What was the purpose of the lie(s), and how did they fit into the case? The evasiveness, fabrications, and deceptions should all be in evidence.

A Brick on the Bedroom Nightstand

On August 2, 2015, at about 3 a.m., a 911 call came in from a home in North Carolina. The caller said that he'd had a fight with his son-in-law, Jason Corbett, and had hit him with a baseball bat. Corbett's wife, Molly, 33, and her father, Tom Martens, 67, admitted to killing Jason. They said they beat Jason in self-defense with a brick paver and a metal baseball bat because Jason was choking Molly and threatening to kill her.

Molly stated that because she felt threatened by her husband, Jason, she recorded the incident on tape. However, she did not reveal the recordings when questioned by police or during the first trial. The existence of the tapes only came to light during the second trial.

With their lives possibly on the line, why didn't Molly bring forward those tapes in the first trial? Was the reason Molly and Tom didn't bring the tapes forward because they were worried about the murder being on tape? And the question is, after consulting with an attorney, did they bring forward all the tapes?

The prevarications in the case began immediately with the interviews of Molly Martens Corbett and Thomas Corbett. They told police that Jason had been drinking, and Tom said that Jason was drunk. This turned out to be a lie. The autopsy showed that Jason was not intoxicated and was even under the driving-impaired limit for alcohol. What Jason did have in his system was some trazodone, an antidepressant and sedative that Molly had a subscription for.

Both Molly and Tom Martens said that there had been a physical fight in the master bedroom that early morning. Molly said that Jason had choked her, and Martens said that he hit Jason with a bat to save his daughter. At one point, Martens said that Jason took the bat away, but he got it back to hit Jason again.

Martens said he had brought the bat to give to Jason's son. He said he was sleeping downstairs when he heard noises above him. He said he grabbed the bat near his bedside and ran upstairs to see what was happening. Martens said that he saw Jason choking Molly and that Jason said he was going to kill her, and that was when he hit Jason with the bat in self-defense.

There were some light marks on Molly's neck and cheek, but Thomas had no injuries at all. An officer repeatedly warned Molly to stop rubbing her neck. This was prior to the photographs of her appearance.

The crime scene was extremely bloody, with blood all around the scene, on the walls, on the floors, on the baseboards, and on the back of a door. There was blood on Molly, on her pajamas, but very little on Martens, who was in a T-shirt and shorts.

Molly said that Jason had been awakened by his daughter's dream, and he was angry so he went after Molly. She said she used a brick that was on the bedroom nightstand to hit Jason. She said she hit him on the head. The brick was found at the scene, and it was covered in blood, hair, and matter. Martens said he didn't see the brick or see Molly hit Jason with it.

Molly said that the children, a young boy and a girl from Jason's first marriage, did not wake up during the incident and were still in their beds. They did not witness any part of the fight.

Martens also said that his wife, Molly's mother, never came upstairs and was never a witness to the incident. If Martens had heard the commotion upstairs, surely Mrs. Martens would have heard something.

Based on the autopsy, the pathologist said that the damage to Jason's head was so severe that he couldn't even determine the precise number of blows he had sustained.

He thought it could have been ten times. There was severe damage on both sides of Jason's head, and his skull was shattered. The pathologist determined that Jason's nose was also broken; he had damage to his face and injuries to his body, legs, and arms. There was also some indication that some of the blows could have been postmortem.

Analysis of the blood spatter patterns at the crime scene showed that, at least at one point, Jason was near the floor when he was struck, as there was blood spray on the lower baseboard and electric outlet.

During the 911 call, the dispatcher guided Tom Martens in giving CPR to Jason. First responders listened to the call and doubted that CPR was really given to Jason based on the counting process and because Martens was not breathless like one usually is after strenuously pressing on someone's chest.

There was some evidence that Jason had been dead for some time before the 911 call. Several of the first responders questioned police about the time frame after the death because of the body temperature. One of the EMTs asked a police sergeant, "How long did they say they waited before they called 911?" She said the body was cool.

The first responders said they thought the blood in the pools of blood was congealed already, and the blood on the walls was starting to dry. Paramedics spoke among themselves, asking when the call was made and what the victims reported about the incident's time frame. They also noted some dried blood on Jason's body.

Analyzing the crime scene, a forensic expert observed several indentations on the walls at various heights where the bat had struck. A typical plastic electric switch plate, near the floor, had blood spatter. Some blood transfers on the wall could have occurred when Jason's head hit the wall. This could have been an indication that the victim was down and close to the floor when hit with the bat.

A police officer photographed both Tom Martens and Molly at the station. The officer said he did not notice any visible injuries on either of them, even though Martens had said that Jason had sent him flying across the room during the fight and Molly claimed Jason was abusing her.

A forensic scientist gave his opinion that, due to the blood spatters on the bed quilt, it was possible that Jason was first hit while he lay in bed. There was a statement that blood found on the inside hem of Martens' shorts indicated that Jason's head was on the floor when hit with the bat. The scientist also pointed out that blood dripping from the vacuum cleaner was splattering to the side, indicating the crime scene had been altered before police arrived.

Jason's sister, Tracey Lynch, said that Molly had told her several fantastic stories about her past. Lynch also said that she learned that Molly had told people she had corresponded with Jason's first wife and that his first wife had died of cancer. Both of these elements were untrue. Molly had contacted Jason Corbett after Jason's first wife had died of an extreme asthma attack and offered to be their nanny. Eventually, Jason and Molly got married and moved from Ireland to North Carolina.

Tracey Lynch also learned that Molly had told several people that she was Jason's daughter's biological mother. Molly had told some people at a gathering that she had given birth to this stepchild, even though some of the people at the party knew otherwise.

During the police interview, both Molly and Martens mentioned that Jason had been abusive. Martens was asked if he had seen any physical abuse, but he said he had not.

Immediately, the police seemed to catch both Molly and Tom in lies about their re-creation of the incident. The police deemed them as not credible when the physical evidence at the crime scene did not corroborate their statements.

The children were interviewed, and it was noted that they used domestic abuse terminology that would not typically be used by young children. They used the terms "verbally and physically abusive" and seemed to have been coached. The judge noted that the children had since recanted; therefore, he would not allow their interviews to be admitted.

Tom Martens also made a statement that he was approached by the father of Jason Corbett's first wife (deceased by the time of the trial), and he said that the father told him he believed Jason had caused the death of his daughter. This fact was contradicted by the father's sworn statement. Another lie?

In his closing arguments, the prosecutor stated that the evidence indicated that Jason had been beaten while close to or on the floor. It was almost impossible that there had been such a big fight yet Tom and Molly had no marks on them. He also stated that Molly was wearing a delicate bracelet that was still intact.

The prosecutor mentioned the fact that Thomas

Martens' hands had no blood on them when paramedics arrived, despite claiming he performed CPR on Jason's blood-soaked chest.

The prosecutor wondered how Martens could not have seen the brick and how Martens' wife did not come up to the disturbance. The prosecutor also pointed out that the paramedics had said that the body was cold, and asked the question, did this mean that there was some time after the killing, and were they staging their story?

In August 2017, Molly Corbett Martens and Thomas Martens were unanimously found guilty of the second-degree murder of Jason Corbett. They were each sentenced to 20 to 25 years in prison.

In 2021, lawyers for Corbett and Martens appealed to the North Carolina Supreme Court for a new trial based on a number of grounds, including that the first jury did not hear the original tapes of the children and on new evidence that Molly had secretly recorded her husband, Jason, yelling and angry.

In March 2021, the North Carolina Supreme Court ruled by a 4–3 majority that they should be granted a new trial. Molly and Martens were released awaiting their new trial.

For the new trial, the children, now much older and aware of the details of the incident, said that they were willing to testify for the prosecution. They then said that Molly coached them to say the things they said in the original interviews.

Before the new trial could begin, in October 2023, both defendants pleaded guilty to a reduced charge of voluntary manslaughter. They were sentenced to 51 to 74 months in prison. Due to the time served, they would serve only 7 more months before being eligible for release.

In the sentencing hearing, the defense presented Jason's alleged verbal abuse of Molly, using the audio evidence of his yelling and anger. They also referred to the taped interviews of the young children.

At that hearing, Jason's now 19-year-old son and 17-year-old daughter gave their impact statements, disputed their earlier statements, and detailed Molly's abuse of them. They urged the judge not to be fooled by Molly (implying her lies).

Did Tom really bring the bat for his grandson or to help overpower Jason? Did Molly start a fight with a drugged husband and use the brick to hit him, or did she use the brick to hit him while he slept? Who would have a brick bedside and not downstairs? Was Molly recording him for divorce proceedings to keep *his* kids (whom she called hers)? Was the murder recorded, and is that why she didn't bring the recordings forward in the first trial? Did Tom and his wife's plans for the evening change when Molly called him about her plans for that night? Did they initiate this incident just prior to any divorce proceedings, when Jason was moving back home, and child custody hearings were pending?

The extensive prevarication, falsehoods, and untruths uncovered in the Jason Corbett case, seemingly not considered in the trial, exhibit a primary feature of the Innocence Machine. Incriminating evidence plus lying should lead to guilt.

This case also reveals a monumental hypocrisy of the innocence system. The Innocence Machine sometimes distorts the search for truth. This is a world where pseudosociology is rampant, an environment where science is ignored. The search for truth appears to have been hijacked by lawyers in the appellate system. Does the appellate system also deserve correction?

Besides, who keeps a brick on their nightstand?

CHAPTER 30

FINAL THOUGHTS ON THE INNOCENCE MACHINE

The innocence system is broken. An out-of-control Innocence Machine is a product of that broken system. Everyone should be skeptical of innocence cases.

The Innocence Machine is based on the assumption that almost everyone who has been convicted *could* be innocent. They start with an over-presumption of innocence. However, the fact remains that most or almost all the people in prison *ARE GUILTY* of the crimes they have committed.

In this book, the aim has been to present both sides of the campaigns to exonerate convicted people, while taking a deep dive into the oversaturation of the innocence craze.

Examining the innocence movement is a delicate task, balancing the good work done by innocence organizations with the potential for the unfounded release of guilty or dangerous criminals. This involves projecting innocence on these convicted people because they claim they are innocent, and that the justice system is flawed, even after being proven guilty.

It is essential that there is a separation of the Innocence Machine from the Innocence Project. The Innocence Project provides valuable and commendable work. However, the Innocence Machine is the craze to seek out and uncover innocent, convicted people, sometimes without thoroughly vetting the case. Sometimes, this review is based on the media and innocence campaigns. As seen in the Porter case, it can be based on the machinations of the convicts themselves. Once the Innocence Machine starts, it becomes a runaway train, unstoppable and out of control.

The Porter case exemplifies the Innocence Machine theme. It demands that all innocence cases be viewed with extreme skepticism. The outcome of that case demonstrates that the siren calls for attention can lead to inappropriate conduct. They can also lead to ignoring specific facts to reach the point of innocence, as seen in many other cases reviewed herein.

The Porter case, the Caldwell case, and several others discussed in this book show that the convict can control the narrative. Still, other cases demonstrate that a public lobbying campaign and a media crusade effectively controlled the narrative, employing a strategy to circumvent incriminating evidence and portray the person as innocent.

This means that in almost all the cases highlighted in this book, innocent activists ignore crucial inculpatory evidence to present the convicted person as innocent.

Just as language is powerful in the courtroom, language is also compelling and influential for the Innocence Machine. Both the prosecution and the defense use language to influence the jury or appellate judges to lean toward their side. Language can also be used in a coercive, deceptive manner. Defense attorneys may use *semantic infiltration*, which is a deceptive smokescreen that changes the words (language) describing the case to minimize certain aspects of evidence and maximize other aspects to try to show the defendant's innocence. Techniques like this may be just belief speaking, in that they sincerely believe the statements they are making. Or they may be purposely *gaslighting* everyone.

Language can take a case and, using the Innocence Machine formula of minimizing evidence and witnesses, disputing DNA and fingerprint evidence, as seen in the cases of Marcellus Williams and Melvin Mikes; whittle it down to a lone witness, as in the Anthony Porter case; shoehorn in an element of police corruption, like in the Karen Read case; or invoke racism like the O. J. Simpson and Julius Jones cases. Add a dash of police incompetence, and for good measure, a SODDI alternate suspect, and the Innocence Machine is off and running.

The language of the innocence crusade is very powerful. Used as a lobbying effort, biased, slanted language, such as "the only witness recanted," can sway judges, governors, and presidents to grant releases and pardons.

It seems that no matter how much cumulative incriminating evidence there is for a convicted murderer, there is always someone who thinks that person is innocent. That's the Innocence Machine. It also seems that true crime enthusiasts and wannabe true crime investigators are scrutinizing every case, hoping the convicted person may actually be innocent.

In this world of true crime obsession, it seems easy for people to bury themselves in the rabbit hole of the Innocence Machine. They accept all the subtly biased language and campaign for the innocence of the imprisoned person. They may then fall into sketchy arguments and speculation about the case, failing to review the evidence from an impersonal clinical perspective.

There should never be a situation where a person is acquitted of a crime based on celebrity, wealth, or high profile. In the same vein as everyone deserves a fair trial, celebrities should be treated with no deference to their social status.

No noble cause should be used to free a murderer. However worthy, it should also not be allowed to color the circumstances in a case such as that of Leonard Peltier.

Reviewing the Innocence Machine's misfires, mistakes, and digressions is not a call to use the concept that "well, he was guilty of something" as an excuse to convict an innocent person. These cases need to be analyzed rationally and objectively, with evidence highlighted.

There appears to be no established policy or procedure for thoroughly vetting and investigating the innocence of individuals who have been convicted of a crime. Who is qualified to do the investigation? Are students, freshly minted lawyers, or interns qualified to conduct these investigations? Certainly not the students in the Porter case. An investigation of these types require a certain uniformity and an impartial, unbiased approach.

Emotion is another factor in the Innocence Machine. It is often the intensity of crime and the perceived horrors of prison that suck people in. It is a normal human emotion that people can have empathy for someone in the terrible position of being in prison for a crime they did not commit — and the concept that, under the right circumstances, almost anyone could end up like that, too. This is commendable, but cannot be combined with rose-colored glasses or blinders to the evidence.

The concern for someone on death row is this emotion on steroids. Death-row cases reach a new level within the Innocence Machine. This is surely warranted because once the sentence is served, there is no turning back the clock. These cases should still be reviewed skeptically.

The ethical and moralistic approach may be based on a desire to instill some normality into a system that seems chaotic. However, innocent activists often have to engage in mental contortions to shape the circumstances and conclude that these people are innocent. There can be a cognitive dissonance between the actual evidence and the evidence that may point to innocence. Activists seem to force a complex narrative to fit what they want to believe, while rejecting a rational view of all the facts of the case.

No innocent person should remain in prison; however, the Innocence Machine seems to foster an environment in which advocating for someone they believe is innocent becomes a noble endeavor. The converse of that mission is the release of truly guilty individuals who continue to commit crimes and prey on our society.

The Innocence Machine can take almost any case and, with the right strategy, marketing, and lobbying, turn it into an innocence project. At least that is the impression we get when these cases are analyzed. Believe the convicted person, minimize incriminating evidence, and promote an innocence campaign using biased language.

The innocent system is obviously broken. Too many people who are provably guilty are being released. There are too many convicts being exonerated who go on to commit crimes after their release. What should we do? What's the solution to this all-encompassing problem?

There should be an accurate accounting of each crime, based on a thorough and objective review of all the evidence. And this should be presented in the case descriptions on social media, and especially the National Registry of Exonerations.

If all the evidence is openly displayed, without any biased language, and it shows there is a chance that the person could be innocent, then that case should proceed in the innocence world. If the defendant's case doesn't make sense, or there is very slim evidence, such as just one eyewitness (truly only one, not created to be one), then the case of innocence perhaps should be pursued.

While everyone in this age of true crime thinks they are great investigators, those conducting the investigations should be vetted for their skills. Perhaps there can be a collaboration with law enforcement. Since most police detectives retire after only 20 years, there should be a sufficient number of ex-detectives available to at least review evidence for innocence organizations. This would also reduce the supposed 42% of cases reviewed by innocence projects as being not wrongfully convicted.

The use of biased language must be recognized and not fostered. Skewed, slanted language will always be emitted from the prisoners themselves and from their families, and then spill out into their supporters. It is the language of the Innocence Machine.

The full aspects of a case, not merely the technicalities as presented in the laundry list of appeals, should be scrutinized in a review. There should be a method to weigh the technicalities and procedures against the inculpatory evidence against the convicted person.

The defendant's verifiable lies should carry equal weight alongside physical and circumstantial evidence.

Judges, appeal courts, governors, and even the president should not allow themselves to be influenced by the hype and the biased language of the Innocence Machine while deciding on pardons and commutations.

It is time to accept that many cases, like the ones presented in this book, have clouded the mission of the innocence organizations and caused many convicted criminals who are guilty to be set free. Some have gone on to commit other crimes, with at least one murdering the person who helped set them free. The cases included in this book are by no means all the cases where this miscarriage of justice has occurred.

No innocent person should remain in prison; however, the Innocence Machine seems to foster an environment in which advocating for someone they believe is innocent, whether they genuinely are, becomes a noble quest worthy of admiration and respect. What gets lost in the nobility of these cases is the truth. Until we see some change in how these investigations are conducted, thoroughly and impartially, without bias or gain, the Innocence Machine will continue to create a travesty of justice from its own flawed actions.

ACKNOWLEDGMENTS

I would like to acknowledge my writing team, Sheila, Evan, Kelye, and Kacie, who provided their support throughout the course of writing all my books. Special thanks to Rick Henning, the "Introduction Master." Rick is a great writing partner.